Cowboys
Talk Right Purty!

by

Edgar "Frosty" Potter

GOLDEN WEST ☼
PUBLISHERS

Cover and text illustrations by Scott Nelson

Includes excerpts from *Cowboy Slang* also written by Frosty Potter and published by Golden West Publishers, Inc.

Library of Congress Cataloging-in-Publication Data
Potter, Edgar R.
Cowboys Talk Right Purty! / by Frosty Potter
    p.   cm.
ISBN 1-885590-00-8
1. Cowboys — West (U.S.) — Language (new words, slang, etc.)
2. Cowboys — West (U.S.) — Slang.   4. Americanisms — West
    (U.S.) I. Title
PE3727.C6P69   1994   94-40725
427'.978'088636 — dc20   CIP

Printed in the United States of America

Information in this book is deemed to be authentic and accurate by author and publisher. However, they disclaim any liability incurred in connection with the use of information appearing in this book.

Golden West Publishers, Inc.
4113 N. Longview Ave.
Phoenix, AZ 85014, USA
(602) 265-4392

Table of Contents

Dedication

This book is dedicated to my son Gordon R. Potter who was killed during World War II in North Africa — 1942.

*Readers of this book . . . Please read this **Foreword** so that you may know what this **Cowboys Talk Right Purty!** is all about!*

Foreword

When I think of all of the slang and dirty words that have crept into our written and spoken language together with the near senselessness of such spelling as knife, knob, lamb, knowledge, wreck, etc., it makes me wonder if it isn't time to throw in the sponge and start all over again?

Is it any wonder that a body must go to school a near fourth of his lifetime in learning to read and write? Should it be necessary that we lug around a ten-pound dictionary to help us talk, write, or say it?

For instance: the word "pretty" in the big two-inch thick Thesaurus book shows 27 other words that mean nearly the same as the word "pretty". I know you won't believe it, but here they are—all twenty-seven of them:

alluring	delicate	nice and round
attractive	engaging	pleasing to the eye
beauteous	fair	shapely
beautiful	fetching	sightly
bonny	good looking	symmetrical
captivating	goodly	well-favored
charming	graceful	well-made
comely	handsome	well-proportioned
dainty	lovely	well-set

As I continued my research I found there to be literally thousands of words with even more multiple meanings than does the word "pretty".

Here are a few: mob has 27, rude has 49, force has 89, help has 39, stand has 89, etc. and don't you suppose I just found that the word "wild" has 117 similar meanings. As you probably wouldn't believe it, here they are:

WILD

abandoned	fanatical	mad	spicy
absorbing	fanciful	madcap	spine-tingling
affecting	fantastic	madly	stimulating
awful	fascinating	maniacal	stirring
awesome	feral	moving	superb
barbaric	ferocious	mythical	tantalizing
berserk	fierce	natural	tempestuous
bizarre	flighty	outlandish	terrible
bleak	foolish	outrageous	thrilling
blustery	forested	overgrown	turbulent
breathtaking	frightful	overpowering	unbroken
captivating	furious	pleasurable	uncivilized
charming	furiously	portentous	uncultivated
choppy	ghastly	preposterous	undisciplined
crazed	giddy	primitive	undomesticated
crazy	gripping	provocative	ungovernable
dazzling	hair-raising	rabid	unhinged
delight	high-flown	raging	uninhibited
delightful	horrible	rampantly	unreal
demented	horrid	rash	unrestrained
desolate	howling	raving	unruly
eerie	illogical	reckless	untamed
elating	ill-advised	riveting	violent
electrifying	impelling	rough	violently
engaging	impractical	rousing	wasted
engrossing	insane	rugged	wildly
enthralling	inspiring	savage	zestful
excessive	lawless	sensational	
exciting	lurid	shocking	
exquisite	macabre	sinister	

Please keep in mind that none of the words involved show or explain the degree, extent, size or scope of the word. Thus, if a man is brave, fat, blind, etc., the listener will want to know how brave, how fat, how blind, etc.

If tall, a cowboy would say "he was half again taller than a bull buffalo", if brave, "would tackle a bobcat bare-handed", if fat, "he was fat in the middle and poor at each end", if blind, "so blind he couldn't see through a bobwire fence", etc. Thus, nearly every word in the English language requires further clarification or amplification.

Hey, let's whoa up a bit and see what all of this talk is about. Just how did the cowboys and stockmen of the old days start using so called slang phrases in connection with their daily work?

Let me tell you how I first became interested! As I recall it was about the year 1906 when I was laid up on our Diamond N Cattle Ranch with a dose of blood poisoning in my off hind leg.

The blood poisoning damn near did me in so Pa had to drive me the 40 odd miles to Mandan to see a sawbones. To keep me from going off my rocker, as Pa says, while I sweat it out he bought me a couple of five cent blood and thunder eight or ten page paperbacks called *"Diamond Dick"*, *"Young Wild West"* and other blood and thunder books.

That's when I first started running down the slang phrases as used by the cowboys. I searched old books such as *Hopalong Cassidy of the Bar-20*, I made up a lot of them myself, got others from ranchers, cowboys and in later years from radio, TV, sermons, newspapers and in fact I may have lifted a few from other books.

By the year 1971 I had about 600 of the phrases on my list. My wife suggested that I write a western oriented book and include the 600 phrases. This was my first book entitled *Cowboy Slang*.

I continued collecting phrases and updating my book and my list soon reached 2,000. During the past couple of years I kept thinking back to the old Chinaman who claimed that "a picture is worth 1,000 words". That thought stuck in my craw as to how a person conjures up a word picture when writing?

To tell your sweetheart that she is pretty is lacking in that she won't know if you mean her face, her legs, hair or whatever. Whereas if the slang word is visioned as a word picture, it could end up as "Rosey, I think you are as purty as a little red heifer in a flower bed."

So in *Cowboy Slang* you will find these beautiful western

phrases such as: *Eyes as black as blackstrap poured on a tin plate ...As sweet and mild as barnyard milk...Pretty as a basket of chips ... Handsome as a new stake rope on a thirty dollar pony.*

Thus with such lavish phrases is it any wonder that the title of my new book had to be *Cowboys Talk Right Purty!*

Beyond a doubt I have come up with a system of talking and writing that will greatly upgrade and modernize our timeworn, cumbersome language of antiquity into a newly inspired and gorgeous modern language that will one day be spoken throughout the civilized world.

No longer will you have to sweat it out wondering which word to use. Simply commit to memory the 2,000 word picture phrases and you may consider yourself a master linguist of the first order.

Critics have indicated that my book *Cowboy Slang* is in a class by itself when it comes to Rodeos, Cowboys, Cattle, Horses, Indians in America, Brands, Bobwire, All Around Champion Cowboys, etc. Just think what a modern up-to-date orator can do with this new revolutionary breakthrough at his command!

Now in this here *new* book of mine, *Cowboys Talk Right Purty,* I have included some more useful and colorful sayin's along with some stories of my growin' up years — you know, on the ranch and all. I've had a pretty interesting life and I figgered I'd share some of it with you. Hey, you know, you're never too old to learn a new trick or two! I've also included some rodeo terms, some horse and cattle info and I've topped it all off with some cowboy poems — some I wrote and some I borrowed (with permission, of course). Thought you might like to see how some of us old-timers entertained ourselves back then!

Now here are some of my favorite cowboy sayings. I shared a lot of these with you in my other book, but I just like these so much I wanted to share them with you again. Besides, some of you reading this here book might not have seen the other book yet!

I'll start with the ladies . . .

Makin' progress!

Women

- There's only two things I'm afraid of, a decent woman an' bein' left afoot.
- Hosses an' wimmin will shore make a man go whistlin', provided he's still young 'nough to pucker.
- She had about as much warmth as an icicle.
- He ordered hisself a wife from a matrimonial agency same as he ordered his under-riggin's.
- The photograph she sent didn't show up all the blemishes.
- The sky-pilot soon had them welded to the neckyoke.
- She soon had him walkin' the fence.
- Soon had 'em hogtied with matrimonial ropes.
- The only evidence of her busband's passin' was the black weeds she cultivated for a week or so.

- That little wisdom-bringer's so sweet the bee trees are gall beside her.
- She soon had him so civilized he'd tote a bumbershoot and wear galluses.
- Yuh can't turn a woman mor'n you can a runaway hog.
- Yuh couldn't a stopped her with a forty-foot rope an' a snubbin' post.
- She was as soft an' fluffy as a goose-hair pillow.
- I'd just as soon marry a orphan asylum.
- In spite of their fancy duds, most of the red-light gals had their hearts in the right place.
- A grass widder is a dangerous critter for a bachelor cowboy.
- She wore so much paint she couldn't even blush.
- She had no trouble gettin' a rake to gather her crop.
- She wasn't even fit for a drinkin' man to hole up with.
- She wasn't wearin' much more than a sneeze an' a ring.
- Their silks an' satins swished till they sounded like a high wind in tall grass.
- She might a had a short rope, but she shore threw a wide loop.

Courting

- He soon had her tied to the snortin' post.
- She soon had him cinched to the last hole.
- Had his tail over the dashboard an' was rarin' to go.
- Range calico was as scarce as sunflowers on a Christmas tree.
- Come a purty gal an' the whole range would be sufferin' Cupid's cramps.
- He called on her as regular as a goose goes barefooted.
- She-stuff can shore make a pealer get his spurs tangled.
- Thet little feller with a bow an' arrer can shore bugger up a cowboy.
- He'd spent his wages on pies an' throat-ticklin' stuff in order to chin with the purty hash-slinger.
- Yuh can't hitch up a horse with a coyote.
- He did hisself some heavy courtin'.
- After she caught him he was plumb lady-broke.

Pretty

- As pretty as a little red heifer in a flowerbed.
- He's so purty I feel like takin' off my hat to him.
- The purtier the gal the worse coffee she makes.
- She was more ornamental than useful.
- Dressed so he looked like a mail order catalog on foot.

- He loomed up like a tin roof on a sunny day.
- Eyes as soft as blackstrap poured on a tin plate.
- As purty as a little red wagon.
- Trim an' neat as a new buggy.
- As prim as a preacher's wife at a prayer meetin'.
- She was as sweet an' mild as barnyard milk.
- As handsome as an ace-full of queens.
- Pretty as a basket of chips.
- Handsome as a new stake-rope on a thirty-dollar pony.

Afraid
- He bolted like a jackrabbit in tall grass.
- Jumped like he'd stepped on a raw egg.
- Jumpin' like a speckled-legged frog from a dry lake.
- A funny feelin' was runnin' up an' down my spine.
- If I'd had bristles I'd a resembled a wild hog.
- Made his skin get up an' crawl all over him.
- It'd make the hair of a buffalo robe stand up.

Awkward
- As awkward as a blind bear in a bramble patch.
- As clumsy as a floundered stud.
- As graceful as an elephant tryin' to use a typewriter.
- As awkward as a bull in a china closet.

Braggart
- He had callouses from pattin' his own back.
- Bragged himself out of a place to lean agin' the bar.
- He throws too much dust.
- He was just a case of big behavior.
- Always lettin' off a little steam.
- Mostly all gurgle an' no guts.
- He was as full of wind as a bull in corn time.

Brave
- Knows how to die standin' up.
- Had more guts than yuh could hang on a fence.
- Had more sand than the Sahara Desert.
- A gent with sand in his craw.
- He'll fight a rattler an' give him first bite.
- Craw jammed plumb full of sand an' fightin' tallow.

Cold

- Coldern' a Montana welldriller.
- As cold as a witch's caress.
- So cold the cows gave icicles.
- Coldern' a knot on the North Pole.
- Colder than hell on a stoker's holiday.
- He was as blue as a whetstone.
- As cold as a dead snake.
- Shakin' like a chihuahua pup with a chill.
- Coldern' frog legs.
- Shiverin' like a lizard lookin' for a hot rock.
- Colder than a mother-in-law's kiss.

Crazy

- As crazy as popcorn on a hot skillet.
- Somebody done stole his rudder.
- Knockin' 'round like a blind dog in a meat market.
- I rekkon the heat kinda addled his think box.
- He was fullgrown in body only.
- As crazy as a parrot eatin' stick candy.
- He was plumb weak north of his ears.
- He was spinnin' 'round like a button on a privy door.
- Crazier'n a locoed bedbug.
- As crazy as a sheepherder.
- He didn't even know where to scratch a hog.
- So narrow-minded he could look through a keyhole with both eyes at the same time.
- Kinda off his mental reservation.
- His intelligence shore ain't in camp.
- If'n yuh bored a hole in his haid yuh wouldn't find 'nough brains to grease a skillet.
- He couldn't sell hacksaw blades in a hoosegow.
- He's now studyin' to be a half-wit.
- When the Lord poured in his brains somebody musta jaggled His arm.

Dumb

- So dumb he couldn't teach a hen to cluck.
- He's as shy of brains as a terrapin is of feathers.
- His brains don't weigh an ounce of ideas to the ton.
- He couldn't cut a lame cow from the shade of a tree.

- All he knows about brains is yuh can buy 'em scrambled.
- He couldn't even drive a nail in a snowbank.
- I'd as soon teach a bull calf to drink as argue with him.
- His brain capacity wouldn't make a drinkin' cup for a hummin' bird.
- He don't know no more than a hog does of a ruffled shirt.
- He ain't got sense 'nough to spit downwind.
- Hasn't got the brains of a grasshopper.
- He musta' been in the basement when they handed out brains.
- Couldn't track an elephant in ten feet of snow.
- Can't tell skunks from housecats.
- Got nothin' under his hat but hair.
- He couldn't track a wagon through a mud puddle.
- As chuckleheaded as a prairie dog.
- He could be plenty ignorant without strugglin' to make a job out of it.
- He couldn't find a bell-cow in his own bed.
- He'd walk into a river so's he could drink standin' up.

Happy
- As expectant as a sparrow watchin' a worm hole.
- Grinnin' like a possum eatin' a yellow jacket.
- As chipper as a couple of jaybirds.
- Grinnin' like a jackass eatin' cactus.
- As happy as a flea in a doghouse.
- Happy as a little kid pullin' a dog's ear.
- As pleased as a little dog with two tails.
- Grinnin' like a skunk eatin' cabbage in the moonlight.
- He was steppin' as high as a blind dog in tall grass.
- Purrin' like a blind cat in a creamery.
- His spirits rose like a corncob in a cistern.

- Like a dead hoss, he ain't kickin'.
- Grinnin' like a weasel peekin' in a henhouse door.

Mad

- So mad he couldn't even bite hisself.
- As prody as a locoed steer.
- As cross as a snappin' turtle.
- Mad 'nough to kick his own dog.
- Fit to be boiled down for glue.
- A screechin' like a plucked jay-bird.
- Mad 'nough to eat the Devil with his horns on.
- So mad he could swallow a horned toad backwards.
- Loaded to the muzzle with rage.
- Sore as a frog on a hot skillet.
- Mad 'nough to kick a hog barefooted.
- Mad as a bear with two cubs an' a sore teat.
- I knocked his jaw back so far he could scratch the back of his neck with his front teeth.
- Stomped out a growlin' to hisself.
- He stood there a filin' his teeth.
- Acted like he was raised on sour milk.
- Humped his back like a hog goin' to war.
- In a sod-pawin', horn tossin' mood.
- A bellerin' like a newmade steer.

Smart

- He was as sure as a cocklebur on a coyote.
- Had more smoke than a wet wood fire.
- Weasel smart he was, too.
- Wise as a tree full of owls.
- Smart as a bunkhouse rat.
- Smart as a cuttin' horse.
- He don't use up all his kindlin' gettin' his fire started.
- He shore has a lot of wrinkles on his horns.
- He don't leave 'nough tracks to trip an ant.
- He knows more about cattle than a rabbit does about runnin'.
- He knows cows, front, back an' sidewise.
- He don't need advice any more'n a steer needs a saddle blanket.
- He's lived in the desert so long he knows all the lizards by their front names.
- As full of information as a mail order catalog.

Rodeo Terms

BICYCLING: The act of scratching with first one foot and then the other in the manner of riding a bicycle *(see scratching)*.

BITING THE DUST: Being thrown from a horse.

BLOWING A STIRRUP: Losing a stirrup, which disualifies rider.

BOGGING THEM IN: When rider fails to scratch horse.

BRONCO: Mexican word for "mean", shortened to bronc or "bronk" in cowboy parlance: a vicious unbroken horse.

BROOMTAIL: Wild mare.

BUCK JUMPING: The gyrations of a bronc in trying to unseat rider.

BULLDOGGER: A steer wrestler.

CANTLE-BOARDING: When the rider scratches back to the cantle. *(see scratching)*

CHAPS: Leather or hair leggings worn by the cowboys to protect their legs.

CROW HOPS: A term contemptously applied to mild bucking motions.

DOG-FALL: Putting a steer down with its feet under him. The throw is not complete until the steer is flat on its side with all four feet out.

EATING GRAVEL: Being thrown from a bucking bronc or wild steer.

FOUR-FOOTING: Catching an animal by the feet with a rope in order to throw same for handling.

GRABBIN' THE APPLE: When a bronc rider grabs the horn of the saddle to keep from being thrown.

COMMUNITY LOOP: Extra large loop thrown by a roper.

HAZER: Steer wrestler's assistant.

HIGH ROLLER: Horse that leaps high in the air when bucking.

HOOLIHANING: The act of leaping forward and alighting on the horns of a steer in bulldogging in a manner to knock the steer down without having to resort to twisting the animal down with a wrestling hold. Hoolihaning is barred at all recognized contests.

LOGGERING: Holding to saddle horn.

PEGGING: When steer wrestler sticks horn into ground. This is not allowed in bulldogging.

PULLING LEATHER: Holding on to saddle with the hand while riding a bucking animal, prohibited by the rules of all contests and scorned by all real cowboys.

SCRATCHING: The act of keeping feet moving in a kicking motion in riding bucking animals, and one of the acts necessary to win at any real contest.

SCREWING DOWN: The act of sinking the spurs into the cinch while riding a bucking horse and failing to scratch as provided in the rules.

SEEING DAYLIGHT: When daylight can be seen between rider and saddle during a bronc ride.

SUN-FISHER: A bucker that twists his body in the air so that sunlight hits his belly.

TIGHT-LEGGING: When rider holds legs tight against horse and does not scratch.

TENDERFOOT: That's what you are if you didn't know the meaning of these words!

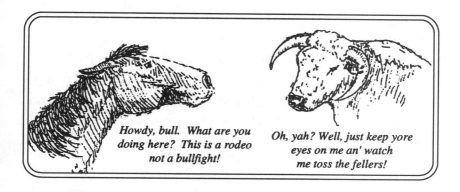

Howdy, bull. What are you doing here? This is a rodeo not a bullfight!

Oh, yah? Well, just keep yore eyes on me an' watch me toss the fellers!

I Shore Like Rodeos!

Rodeos, taken from the Spanish "rodear" have been around for over 100 years. But how do we know that back a few hundred or even a thousand years a few of the boys wouldn't get together and kick up their heels and ride whatever critter they had available to vie with each other for the hand of a fair maiden?

Several locals claim the honor of having put on the first rodeo. One of the earliest seems to have been a bronc ridin' contest between a couple of ranches in the neighborhood of Deer Trail, Colorado as early as 1869. In 1872, Cheyenne, Wyoming was the scene of a Texas steer and bronc ridin' contest.

By this time business was startin' to pick up and in the early 1880's several of the local ranches held steer roping contests on the main street of Pecos, Texas with the court house yard bein' used as a corral. Even though there was no charge made to watch the show, they have made it stick that this was the first official rodeo.

Then along in 1888 Prescott, Arizona put on what they still call the "Grand-daddy of 'em all" where prizes were awarded and admission charged. They claim it is the oldest continual annual rodeo in America and have the oldest known trophy to prove it.

Miles City in Montana came along in 1891. Cheyenne, Wyoming with their Frontier Days in 1897, the Pendleton Roundup in 1911, and the Calgary Stampede in Alberta, Canada in 1912. From then on things really started to move, making rodeos - in my opinion - the best loved entertainment of all national sports.

By then rodeos were getting to be big business and in 1929 the management of several leading rodeos organized the Rodeo Association of America. Then to protect their interests, rodeo participants banded themselves together as the Cowboy's Turtle Association. In 1945 the Turtles changed their name to Rodeo Cowboys Association and finally in 1945 to the Professional Rodeo Cowboys Association, composed of contestants and former contestants to regulate all aspects of the rodeos.

In the old days if a feller was a rancher we knew he was a cow rancher. But nowadays there are so damn many kinds of ranches yuh have to ask "what kind of a ranch?" Why they run the gamut all the way from chicken ranches, hog ranches, fruit ranches, vegetable ranches to dude ranches and ad infinitum (that word shore made me sweat).

And now that I am in such a peaceful sod-pawin' horn tossin' mood, I might add that up to fairly recent a rodeo was a rodeo. Now there's another critter in the picture called a gymkhana. Don't ask me to pronounce it 'cause it took me quite a while before I would even buy me a ticket. But a few gymkhana's under my belt and I had to admit that they stack up right along with a regular rodeo. Could be though that if both of them were called a rodeo it might give the word rodeo a little more clout. In case yuh don't already know it, back as far as forty years ago there were better' than 1,000 or 1,500 rodeos including just the fair to middlin' sizes. These are over and above the small towns and hamlets with maybe just a half dozen or more cowpokes lettin' off a little steam on their way home from church.

And all that was forty or fifty years ago mind you. During past years rodeos have leaped ahead of most other sports. Even when I was still on the ranch across from the reservation, if we went down on the reservation to see a friend (or maybe steal a pony) we would probably run across a rodeo or two. And you'd better believe them fellers knew how to put on a rodeo. I'm talkin' back in 19 aught 5 or 1910 or better when few of the Indians had saddles. Maybe we could top 'em ridin' a bronc with a saddle, but at ridin' bareback and doin' a few tricks, they shore had us licked.

So now with thousands of rodeos scattered around the country, the attendance by folks is near fantastic. Yup, rodeos will continue to be a popular event. I have always figured that a rodeo gives a feller more entertainment to the square inch than any of the other sports such as baseball an' such and even horse racin' which draws about the most folks.

Now don't think for a moment that ridin' a rodeo circuit is a bed of roses. No sir, them boys earn their salt and then some. The more rodeos they hit and events they enter along with their own favorite and higher paying events, determine their annual take. And don't get the idea that the take is net! Not by a jug full it ain't.

During the rodeo season they are on the move day and night going from one rodeo to another, sometimes two in one day. They travel by bus, camper, truck-drawn horse trailer and even in their own plane should they own one. They think nothing of traveling 500 or more miles between drinks, 'er I mean rodeos and will flop wherever they can find room to lay down. About the only stock they haul around is their favorite roper or cuttin' horse. Buckin' stock, bulls an' such are usually furnished by the stock owner.

There was a time when most of the participants were bonafide cowboys fresh off the range. Who are they now? Hard to say as they run from "dyed in the wool" cowboys to school teachers, doctors, and clerks to college and university students in many walks of life. Fix any of them up with a pair of Levi's, a ten gallon hat, carved leather belt with an ornate buckle, a denim shirt along with a pair of boots and you can scarcely tell them apart. But put fifty of 'em together and ask the real McCoys to stand in one group, and the entire 49 or even all 50 of them will scatter like a bunch of chickens with a hen hawk overhead.

I might say that there are a few dead giveaways you might

watch in yore dress such as: don't tuck the legs of yore pants into the top of yore boots, don't turn up the bottom of yore pants a couple of inches (which a few years back was used to flick the ash on yore cigarette into the cuff rather than to feel the wrath of the lady should yuh do yore flickin' on her freshly polished floor or Burmese carpet), by all means don't scratch yore matches across the seat of yore pants if yore self-commencer lighter don't work, of course should she loan you hers be sure you return it to her) don't wear a short sleeve shirt, and do keep a short hair cut.

Closest he's been to a cow is a T-bone steak!

Now with tickets in hand let's find us a seat in the grandstand if you can afford it, or in the bleachers or "rush seats" as I call 'em. The sun can get awful hot or rain awful wet, so get under the roof if you can 'cause the arena activities usually continue despite the weather. Cowboys and cowgirls will near crawl around in six inches of mud, or be drug through the mud until they look like ruttin' boars in a mud hole.

Like I was going to say, get seats as close as yuh can to the ropin' gate. That's where most of the action is and you'll get a good view of the ropin' and bulldoggin' and be close to where horse races end.

Now at long last after havin' set the better part of an hour on a hard seat we are ready to watch the big show, 'er, well not quite, as the announcer has got to check the volume of the loud speakers and take a few minutes to kid with the clowns a bit or even have them put on a smallish dog show for us.

Suddenly and unexpectedly a dynamite bomb explodes overhead telling all and sundry that the show is about to commence. With our nerves at near breakin' point, loud speakers turned up to their highest pitch, the band breaks into John Phillip Sousa's world famous Charge of the Light (horse) Brigade. We all come to our feet as a speedin' horseman comes dashin' into the arena carrying the American flag. By this time us fellers wearin' hats are holdin' them up near our hearts while the rest of the folks cross one arm across their chest. We continue to stand up while someone sings the Star Spangled Banner, our national anthem.

Then with the band pickin' up speed and volume, here comes the Grand Entry parade. The queen with her escorts, stock contractor with his pickup men, and you won't believe how many officials and just common dignitary folks get into the parade. All dressed in their finest, riding beautiful horses, near makes us want to climb down out of our hard seats and join in the parade. Not a bad idea, is it?

The din is terrific as the parade circles the arena. Finally certain dignitaries are introduced by name as they madly gallop and line up in front of the grandstand as they come to a near dead stop. The men folks, polite as usual, doff their hats or wave a hand, while the ladies and gals resort to their own special brand of greeting best designed to get the most mileage.

Now, if all of this pomp and splendor hasn't caused yore adrenaline to start flowin' yuh might as wella' stayed home. Just one thing more before things start to commence. The announcer wants to introduce the stock furnisher and the two pickup men and probably the clowns, and might even induce the clowns into putting on a small act with a trained mule or dog or something. Usually those acts are pretty good.

Now I am sure we're ready as the announcer says, "Ladies and gentlemen, I now give you Bill Hooker of Acme, Wyoming coming out of chute 3 on Snowflake, a world famous bucker." We hurriedly look for chute 3 and maybe turn to our seat pardner and ask "What

name did he say?" Well, by that time the bronc and rider have long since left the chute and are halfway down the arena as the whistle blows. Those 8 seconds went by so fast you didn't even see the ride, did you? I don't blame you much as I too have often wished that the announcer would mention the chute number at the start of his spiel so that we could at least locate chute 3 in time to see the bronc and rider come out. There's usually plenty of action as the bronc makes his first move out of the chute.

That's what I like about a rodeo, every time a gate opens you can expect a tornado or something in the form of a critter to come out squeelin' and abellerin' with fire in its eye and asnortin' fire an' brimstone at every jump. The fact that the rider has to keep one arm in the air doesn't simplify the ride in any way inasmuch as he would give a leg if he could reach down with that arm and grab the nubbin' - of which there ain't none on a buckin' saddle.

So far I've only mentioned saddle bronc riding. How about all those other events such as bareback bronc riding, bull dogging, calf roping, barrel racing, team roping, bull riding, steer roping and wrestling, and the rough stock events, to say nothing of the clowns cuttin' up. Besides that there's even wild hoss ridin' and old folks ridin' a hoss bareback.

I was thinking of going on to another subject, but I'll take the time to talk to you about bull riding.

So now let's watch a cowboy ride a big overgrown 2,000 pounds or more of blood and guts that goes by the ladylike name of Brahma. Them big fellers with a hump on their neck have got snake blood in their veins and they are about as sociable as an ulcerated back tooth. Why, they will hide behind a fence post all day just waitin' to tromp on, disembowel, or at least toss a feller into the next county. The rider hangs on to a single rope around a bull's belly. The other hand is free but may not touch any part of the bull or his own self.

One time I was sittin' on a ten foot high fence taking pictures when one of them big fellers wanted out, and usin' me for a target cleared the fence, and his wind, as he went by, took me with him with my camera on top.

Bull riding is the most dangerous of the several events, yet more cowboys choose this event than any other. One or more clowns are always near the rider and should the rider be thrown, it is up to the clowns to divert the attention of the bull before he horns or tromps on a rider. When thrown, the rider has all of a half to three quarters of a second to either run like hell, climb the fence or likely be horned and boosted over the fence by the irate bull.

On occasion a rider's hand can become caught in a twisted rope. Bulls are quick to take advantage of it and attempt, by spinning, to smash a rider's head against a post or tromp him to death. The clowns must be nimble footed or hide in a rubber barrel. A good show is put on when a clown gets down on his hands and knees and paws dirt to make the bull mad. He usually succeeds to the point that he, in his efforts, starts looking for a vacant barrel. I am pretty sure that you won't fall asleep watching a bull ride.

But whatever happens, you don't see no handshakin' or kissin' each other by the cowboys. He don't want to be nurse maided by having someone pick up his hat, help him stagger to his feet or help him high tail it to the nearest fence. Oh, of course, if he had a broken leg or arm or something, why sure, somebody might come out and wrap a bandana or piggin' string around his sore so he could be ready for his next go-'round. The cowboys, however, are a kindly lot as should a fellow rider get full killed they always make it a point to write to his wife and ask where she would like to have his saddle sent and tell her, as gently as possible, that her husband got killed ridin' a bull.

But like I said at the start, there ain't anything better for fun and excitement than a good old rodeo.

YUP, I SHORE LIKE RODEOS!

Rodeo Sayin's

Bronc Riders

- He went sailin' off — his hind laigs kickin' in the air like a migratin' bullfrog.
- He et gravel without stoopin'.
- That hoss throwed him clean into a funeral parlor.
- There's a heap more to bein' a rider than just settin' on a hoss an' lettin' yore feet hang down.
- Yuh got throwed so high I was lookin' to see if St. Peter had whittled his initials in yore boot soles.
- I shore was achin' in a lot of new places.
- I was knockin' a hole in my chest with my chin.
- After three jumps he hit the ground and laid still.
- He got up with three handfuls of something he didn't want.
- All I could do was just aim to run down his mainspring.
- He left his hoss in an unscheduled flight.
- The cantle of the saddle hit me in the caboose an' I started for a flight to Mars.
- Throwed me further than a Death Valley buzzard can smell a dry canteen.
- Thet hoss looked as easy as shootin' fish in a dry lake.
- He could stomp yuh into the ground so deep you'd take root an' sprout.
- I didn't break nothin', but all my hinges, bolts an' nuts was shore loosened.
- I got throwed so high I could've said my prayers before I lit.
- He was clawin' leather by the handfulls.
- For a minute I thought I'd mounted backward as I shore in hell couldn't find his haid.
- I soared so high it was damn scary without wings.
- He stuck like a tick in a lamb's tail.
- Yuh couldn't a chopped him loose from thet hoss with an axe.
- He screwed hisself down in the saddle an' stuck like a postage stamp.
- He couldn't ride nothin' wildern' a wheel-chair.
- After that ride all I needed to make me a cripple was a tin cup an' a handful of pencils.
- That hoss soon had 'em pickin' daisies.

- Just keep one leg on each side an' yore mind in the middle.
- He couldn't ride a rail fence in a stiff breeze.

Horses (buckin')
- Hoss acted like he was a tryin' to chin the moon.
- Thet hoss hid his head an' kicked the lid off.
- That roan could buck off a man's whiskers.
- Hoss was a showin' his belly like he was proud of it.
- Arched his back like a mule in a hailstorm.
- The hoss just sinks his haid an' unloads him.
- He pitched as stiff-legged as a mad ostrich.
- That hoss couldn't throw off a wet blanket.

Horses (cuttin')
- He can turn on a biscuit an' never break the crust.
- Says his hoss can turn through the eye of a needle.
- He can turn on a button an' never scratch it.
- That bay of mine can cut a gopher from his hole.
- He could cut fly-specks from a can of pepper.
- He can turn on a quarter an' leave 'nough change to buy a can of beer.
- My hoss will stick to a calf like a burr on a sheep's tail.

Horses (usin')
- So genteel yuh could stake him on a hairpin.
- That old hoss is dead, but he just won't lay down.
- Rode him till he was covered with lather like a barber had prepared him for a shave.
- He fogs up to the snortin' pole an' spikes his hoss's tail.
- His hoss was leadin' the race like an antelope would a hog.
- He was throwin' dirt in the eyes of a jackrabbit.
- Was a foggin' down the road like he's going to a dance.
- He punched the breeze an' traveled faster'n bad news at a church social.
- He shore was a skippin' through the dew.
- If he humps hisself much more, he'll shore set his belly a smokin'.
- He humped his tail at the shore-end an' made far apart tracks.
- He was movin' faster'n a squirrel in a cage.
- He was goin' like the clatter-wheels of hell.
- He starts for hell-an-gone an' forty miles beyond.
- His shadow was always twenty minutes behind him.

Bareback Bronc Riding

Lots of folks nowadays strap a Sears Roebuck saddle on a pony, climb up the side with an apple box to help them an' figure they are a cowboy. Or they might even get on bareback an' figure they are set to ride in a rodeo. But little do they know what it is like to climb a raw bronc with just a rope around the horse belly to hang on to.

There are no stirrups to absorb the jolts from the stiff-legged leaps and no buck rein to help keep his balance. The cowboy gets a zero if his spurs are not over the bronc's shoulders when the bronc's feet hit the ground on the first leap out of the chute.

Extra credit is given for spurring over the shoulders, but the cowboy's legs are usually waving in the air like a migrating bullfrog and he can't get his legs down that far. All it takes is eight seconds to win. But after the first few seconds the cowboy is probably numb all over and don't know or give a damn if he has been ridin' eight seconds or eight minutes.

As you watch, you wonder why his neck hasn't been snapped off. But lately some cowboys avoid this neck snappin' by layin' near flat on the horse's rump. Maybe this is just a ploy to ketch themselves a little nap - of the unconscious kind, I mean. All this time the cowboy must have one hand in the air.

Each of the two judges score the cowboy and the bronc separately from 1 to 25 points. All four figures added together could equal 100 points, which is rarely (if ever) reached.

Bull Riding

Some folks like to commit suicide by jumping in the creek or by swallowing some coyote poisoning. But if you want excitement, try ridin' a wild bull.

He will find himself astride a near ton of twisting, pounding, sky-rocketing muscle, bone and guts. Whether the bull is a spinner or a high kicker, the cowboy knows that he is near putting his life on the line, or at least sticking his neck way out.

Even if the cowboy can stay on the full eight seconds, he's still got the big job of gettin' out of the arena in one piece before those vicious horns can disembowel him, cram his teeth down his gullet and probably stomp on him besides. Fortunately there is always a colorful clown or clowns who are willing to risk their lives when necessary to lure the bull from the fallen rider.

All the rider has to hang on to is a rope around the bull's body behind the hump. A loop in the rope enables the cowboy to near wedge his gloved hand under the rope - not too tight, however, as frequently when the rider gets throwed, his hand becomes stuck under the rope and the rider becomes a spinning projectile to be slammed against a wall or corral post. When this happens, cowboys as well as clowns literally crawl all over the bull to free the cowboy. Yes, I can say without question that bull ridin' will give you the greatest eight second excitement of any of the known sports.

Each of the two judges score the cowboy and the bull separately from 1 to 25 points for the rider, and the bull easily earns himself another 1 to 25 points for his own humble effort. Unlike other riding events, the bull rider does not have to spur his bull, which is just as well as he is kept fairly busy just trying to keep his seat, let alone having other chores to look after.

The rider is disqualified if bucked off, if he touches equipment or his person or bull with his other hand, if he uses sharp spurs, or places spurs or edge of chaps under the rope when the rope is being tightened.

Calf Roping

In calf roping yore only partner is a damn well-trained horse. When the barrier goes down, the calf takes off like a cut cat with the horse leaping out after him.

A neck catch and the horse near buries its tail in the ground in a sudden stop as the rider fades from the horse, runs down the rope, throws the calf and ties up three wildly kicking legs. What a thrill it is to watch the horse as he breaks into a dead run on the first jump, how he follows the calf in just the right position for the rider to make his throw, how he slides to a stop when the calf is caught, how he backs, if necessary, to keep the rope tight while the rider goes down the rope, throws the calf and makes the tie.

If the calf is jerked down when caught, it must be allowed to get to its feet before being thrown for the tie. The calf may be tied by crossing any three legs and the tie must hold for six seconds.

I always figger that calf roping is the smoothest and fastest action of all arena events. The calves weigh from 200 to maybe 350 pounds depending upon breed and age. Believe me, they are all as fast as chain-lightnin' from the chute to the cowboy's throw.

As the horse's tail hits the ground, so does the cowboy and he is halfway down the rope before the calf hits it. Notice the apparent ease with which the cowboy lifts 2 or 3 hundred pounds of fighting and bellerin' son of a catamount with one hand in the flank and the other grabbin' a handful of hair as he slams it to the ground. In less than a second he has slipped the loop of the six-foot peggin' string (carried between his teeth) over the top front leg, pulled up the two kickin' hind legs, made a couple of turns and a half-hitch and raises his arms that the job is done.

Wow - now I tell you that's fast! Why most folks in the settin' seats don't usually even get their eyes focused before the job is done.

Is it any wonder that the owner of a well-trained calf ropin' horse practically eats and sleeps with his hoss? Next time you watch this event, keep yore eyes on the hoss. The cowboy will do his part but he might as well go back to bed was it not for his hoss.

Watch the sparkle in the hoss' eye as he near dances for joy as he keeps the rope at the right tension, or maybe backs up a foot or so as the calf struggles. Oh, he might get a little rambunctious and drag the calf a few inches an' get a handful of dirt throwed at him, but he knows darn well that most of the applause was for him as all the cowboy had to do was tie up three legs of the calf.

I remember one time after a particularly fast tie, the cowboy made himself a graceful bow and I near fainted when the horse lifted one front leg and bent his head near to the ground.

Saddle Bronc Riding

Saddle bronc riding takes a man with hair on his chest if any rodeo event does. Eight seconds of vicious violence — much less if the bronc wins!

Setting on the hurricane deck of a rough one you will probably think that you have split at the crotch, your liver has turned over, and your eyeballs bulge as you near enter a coma waiting for the ground to come up so you can "eat dirt without stoopin'" or to hear the raucous whistle of the judge.

By this time you are ready to welcome the loving arms of the pickup man and hit ground, grin sheepishly at the cheering crowd, pick up yore hat and with one hand holding yore rump, limp painfully from the arena. Should you ask the cowboy how he enjoyed the ride he will probably admit to aches in a lot of new places and that "quite a few nuts an' bolts have been loosened".

All broncs are furnished by the stock contractor and each cowboy's bronc is selected by a judge drawing a number out of a hat. Big broncs are the choice of the cowboys as a large horse is more powerful and can usually put up a better fight.

In saddle bronc riding a special regulation saddle is used which is simply a trimmed-down Western saddle but lacks a horn. The horse wears a halter with a single braided rope which the rider holds in his hand on the same side of the halter to which it is attached. A sheep lined leather bucking strap is tightened around the horse's flank to make the horse buck harder, and it sure does.

Spurring is a must and plays a large part in the scoring of the judges. Rider is required to have his spurs high in the base of the bronc's neck and hold them there until the bronc's front feet hit the ground outside of the chute. If he doesn't spur his bronc out of the chute, his ride is forfeited. Saddles are usually furnished by the stock contractor or by the rider if they meet the strict specifications.

Cowboys must hold one hand in the air, with the other holding the buck rein. Rider can be disqualified for pulling leather, changing hands on the rein, wrapping the rein around his hand, losing his stirrup or by touching the animal or equipment with his freehand.

Each of the two judges score the cowboy and the bronc separately from 1 to 25 points. All four figures added together could equal 100, which is seldom, if ever, reached.

Powder River let 'er buck!

Steer Roping

That's easy, I can do that myself, but the roping is only a small part of the event which calls for throwing and tying the critter.

On open ranges before the advent of corrals and chutes and such, if a full grown steer had to be throwed to be doctored, etc., it was up to the cowboy to single handed throw the critter. Even now at rodeos only a powerful man and an oversize horse will attempt this event.

Rodeo rules provide that steers must be caught by both horns only. When catch is made the steer will usually continue running straight ahead. With slack in his rope, the cowboy can with an up and down motion of his rope, cause it to rise and it can be flipped over the steer's right hip and slide down to its knee or hock.

The cowboy then races ahead and to the left so that the tightened rope will jerk the steer's hind feet from under it. Even if the rope is higher up near the tail area, it will turn the steer end for end and usually jerk it to the ground.

Now that we have the steer down, how long will it stay down while the cowboy ties three legs together? I might as well admit that I don't have the foggiest idea what the steer, hoss or cowboy will do under the circumstances. I do know that a steer is not about to stay laid down while the cowboy ties three legs together. It's going to take some pretty fast action for the cowboy to run down the rope and hope that his extra super-trained horse, even with near human sense of judgement, holds the critter to the ground while the rider ties up three legs.

An 800 pound steer is not like a 200 pound calf that the cowboy can pick up and slam to the ground. I've seen such steers kick a dog 10 feet when it tried to sneak in to nibble a hock. It must take brute strength to get such an enraged maddened critter's three legs all in a bunch to make a tie. To hold a calf, the hoss need only back up a foot or so. To hold a steer on the ground requires that the hoss keep tension to keep the hind legs drawn up close to the front feet. If there is such a hoss, I would shore admire to own it.

Steer Wrestling
Bull Dogging

Now here's a good sample exercise should yuh feel you've just got to tackle something that scares hell out of the mere thought of even tackling the steer. Course yuh got to have a little help here to keep the critter runnin' in a straight line.

As soon as the barrier drops, the steer gets a teeny bit head start down the arena and the "dogger" drops out of the saddle onto the head of the steer and digs in his boot heels to slow him up as he tries to twist the steer down. Sounds easy, but it's about as dangerous as kickin' a loaded polecat. A flick of the steer's head could poke a long horn into yore eye quickerin' an old maid can crawl under a bed. Nope, when I want to tango, it won't be with a half-ton steer.

When the steer is flat on its side with all four feet and head straight, time is taken. If the steer goes down the wrong way, the cowboy must let him up and try again. Should the steer get loose after he is jumped on, the cowboy can take only one step to regain his hold. But before the cowboy can take that step, the steer is usually long gone. Time is taken from the opening of the gate 'til the cowboy raises his arms that the job is done.

Bulldoggin' as it is commonly called nowdays is a hair raisin' event in its own right. Back around the 1880's bulldogs were used to catch a steer by the upper lip and throw it to the ground, or at least hold it until the cowboy could take over.

In 1881 a big cowboy on a ranch in Texas figured he could do the same as the bulldog. He was successful and later gained great notoriety in exhibitions with the famous *101 Ranch Wild West Show*. The all time record of bulldoggin' was won by my friend Oral Zumwalt of Missoula, Montana in 2.2 seconds.

Team Roping

As one feller can only rope one end of a cow critter at the same time, he's got to have a partner. As with calf roping, this is rapid fire operation with split second timing. As the catch is made each cowboy must dally his rope and hold in that manner.

Each cowboy's part in the operation seems to be cut and dried making it look almost like a square dance where you allemande left with a sashay or two. It should surely be set to music.

As the gate opens, the steer heads for the wide open spaces pursued by a "header" and a "heeler". Header on the left, heeler on the right. Header throws his rope catching steer by both horns, around the neck or neck and one horn. Now the dance begins. Header sashays his horse sharply to the left which pulls the steer's front end to the left with its back end handily exposed so that the heeler can throw his loop low and under the steer's belly hoping to pick up both hind legs.

Sounds simple don't it? But wait, should the header accidentally catch a front leg along with the head, the team is penalized five seconds. Or should the heeler catch only one hind leg, or if one or both legs are caught above the hocks, they are again fined a five second penalty.

If things went well they now back their horses facing each other with the steer stretched between them. The steer must still be on its feet with the ropes stretched fairly tight.

The horses then bend a knee in curtsy and with a light bow of the head, accept adoration of the wildly cheering crowd. The cowboys likewise raise their hands in greeting and to advise that the job is complete and time may be taken.

Barrel Racing

Cowgirls - makes me shiver just to think of them. "Purty as a little red heifer in a flower bed". Everything in the right place an' dogged out in the duds that are really "flashiarity" to behold.

Certain men folks figure they are only good for barrel racing. Hells fire, I once knowed a couple of gals who lived over near the Yellowstone Park as could ride anything with hair on. One of them's name was Margery somethin' or other and could she ride !!

In barrel racing three barrels are set in a triangle and the rider must circle the barrels against time. A judge drops a flag as the rider starts the run and again as she comes back across the line. If the horse and rider knock over a barrel they will be penalized 10 seconds. This, of course, makes it almost impossible to turn in a good time.

Only highly bred fast horses stand any chance in this fast action event. While riders don't exactly have to be highly bred, they do have to be darn good riders to hang on during the hairpin turns so sharp that at times a stirrup will nearly touch the ground. As the rider makes the last turn and heads for home with her quirt playing a tattoo on the side of her bronc, she gets plenty of encouragement from the folks up in the settin' stands, believe me now.

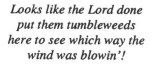

Looks like the Lord done put them tumbleweeds here to see which way the wind was blowin'!

Rodeo Rough Stock Events

If the average rodeo doesn't furnish enough excitement to satisfy you, let me say that there are near another dozen events. Some you will find only very rarely. Others are even more exciting and even more dangerous than the usual seven events you will see at most rodeos. This book is already getting too big so I will just give you a brief picture of the so called "other events".

WILD HORSE RACE

Let's start with the Wild Horse Race which by itself has all of the excitement and danger as some of the smaller standard events. Two or more of the toughest, wildest, orneriest outlaw critters in the west are led into the arena. Three cowboys, two of them called "muggers", and a rider handle each horse. The two damn fool "muggers" attempt to manhandle the outlaw critter with their bare hands. I've seen a cowboy grab an outlaw around the neck and be tossed ten feet in the air. When a saddle is cinched down, the ridin' cowboy has got to first get on, and then race around the track in an aforehand stated direction. The first outlaw around the track is the winner. Time usually runs from five minutes to two hours, in which case weaker gutted audiences usually call it a day and head for home.

CHUCK WAGON RACE

Next in thrills is surely the Chuck Wagon Race. Four horses are hitched to stripped down chuck wagons. Two or three mounted cowboys are called "outriders". At the sound of a gun one of the outriders throws a fifty pound cook stove and a tent and tent poles into the back of his wagon. Now picture three or four horse outfits in the arena! At the sound of a gun each outfit must execute a tight figure eight in the arena. How they keep from smashing into each other is a miracle, and believe me they do smash into each other at times. After making the figure eight they take off at breakneck speed with the outriders doing their best to urge the team to their top speed. The first wagon around the track is the winner. If you want excitement — here it is.

WILD COW MILKING

Wild Cow Milking furnishes a lot of humor. Several range cows are put into the arena and cowboys, each armed with a small baby feeding bottle try to get enough milk that can be poured from the bottle. A lot of humor enters the picture when a clown from the corner of the arena appears and tries to get milk from his cow, which turns out to be a bull.

HIDE RACE

A prime favorite of mine is a Hide Race. A hide is just a flat cowhide that has laid in the sun 'til near brittle. Cowboys on horses drag cowhides on the end of a rope at top speed past the grandstand. As the hide goes past, some feller with guts flops himself belly down, flat on the hide and hangs on for dear life. You can imagine the dust and sh..., well I won't say it, but imagine what they have near got to eat as they go whizzin' by.

DINNER BELL DERBY

The Dinner Bell Derby. A half dozen or more colts and their mothers are kept in different pens until the colts are real hungry. The mares are put in one end of the arena and the colts in the other end. When the gate opens, the first colt to run down the length of the arena and grab a teat of his ma gets a pretty red ribbon tied to its tail. Lots of fun.

AND . . . THERE'S MORE!

Then there's Wild Cow Racin', and Shetland Pony Buckin' for kids, as well as riding such animals as yak, buffalo and such. There's boys and senior citizens bronc riding, quarter horse racing, Roman riding racing, relay races, breakaway for old men and kids, junior dally ribbon roping, flag racing for boys, obstacle races for girls, pole bending and goat tying. I ain't even mentioned parades yet, but I'm going to stop. At least I've given you a good idea of some of the events at a rodeo.

Thet cow may be a mother, but she shore ain't no lady!

I'll put my money on the dog!

Rodeo Rules

When you attend a rodeo and are not familiar with rules to protect the treatment of the animals, you are likely to think that they are being treated in an inhumane manner. Such is not the case but I would like to further assure you on this point so I decided to give you the rules as taken from the rodeo rules book. So don't you worry about those little calf fellers. They are well able to care for themselves. They sure can kick and more than one cowboy has gotten a lightning fast kick alongside of his jaw.

RULES

1. No locked rowels, or rowels that will lock on spurs, or sharpened spurs may be used on bareback horses or saddle horses.
2. Cowboy must adjust rope and reins in such a manner that will prevent horse from dragging calf.
3. The placing of fingers in eyes, lips, or nose of steers while wrestling is forbidden.
4. No animal shall be beaten, mutilated, or cruelly prodded. Standard prods shall be used as little as possible. Animal shall be touched only on hip or shoulder area with the prod.
5. No stimulants or hypnotics to be used or given to any animal used for contest purposes.
6. Chutes must be so constructed as to prevent injury to stock.
7. Clowns are not to abuse stock in any fashion.
8. Use of fireworks to frighten animals is prohibited.
9. Any animal that becomes excessively excited so that it gets down in the chute repeatedly, or tries repeatedly to jump out of the chute, or in any way appears to be in danger of injuring itself should be released immediately.
10. Any PRCA member, including stock contractor, guilty of mistreatment of livestock may be fined not to exceed $500.00.
11. The PRCA shall invite sponsors to invite representatives of the Humane Association to inspect all livestock and the handling of animals.

Rodeo Cowboy
All-Around Champions

Year	Cowboy	Money Won
1959	Jim Shoulders, Henryetta, OK	$ 32,905
1960	Harry Tompkins, Dublin, TX	32,532
1961	Benny Reynolds	31,309
1962	Tom Nesmith, Bethel, OK	32,511
1963	Dean Oliver, Boise, ID	31,329
1964	Dean Oliver, Boise, ID	31,150
1965	Dean Oliver, Boise, ID	33,163
1966	Larry Mahan, Brooks, OR	40,358
1967	Larry Mahan, Brooks, OR	51,996
1968	Larry Mahan, Salem, OR	49,129
1969	Larry Mahan, Brooks, OR	57,726
1970	Larry Mahan, Brooks, OR	41,493
1971	Phil Lyne, George West, TX	49,245
1972	Phil Lyne, George West, TX	60,852
1973	Larry Mahan, Dallas, TX	64,447
1974	Tom Ferguson, Miami, OK	66,929
1975	Tom Ferguson, Miami, OK	50,300
1976	Tom Ferguson, Miami, OK	87,908
1977	Tom Ferguson, Miami, OK	76,730
1978	Tom Ferguson, Miami, OK	103,734
1979	Tom Ferguson, Miami, OK	96,272
1980	Paul Tierney, Rapid City, SD	105,569
1981	Jimmie Cooper, Monument, NM	105,861
1982	Chris Lybbert, Coyote, CA	123,709
1983	Roy Cooper, Durant, OK	153,391
1984	Dee Pickett, Caldwell, ID	122,618
1985	Lewis Feild, Elk Ridge, UT	130,347
1986	Lewis Feild, Elk Ridge, UT	166,042
1987	Lewis Feild, Elk Ridge, UT	144,335
1988	Dave Appleton, Arlington, TX	121,546
1989	Ty Murray, Stephenville, TX	134,806
1990	Ty Murray, Stephenville, TX	213,772
1991	Ty Murray, Stephenville, TX	244,231
1992	Ty Murray, Stephenville, TX	225,992
1993	Ty Murray, Stephenville, TX	297,896
1994	Ty Murray, Stephenville, TX	246,170

Cowboy Horse Sense

*Or, how a cowboy might describe his own
(or someone else's) horse.*

Bangtail
Boneyard
Bronco
Broomtail
Bucker
Buzzard Bait
Calf Horse
Carvin' Horse
Cayouse
Circle Horse
Colt
Cow Horse
Coy Pony
Crowbait
Cutt'n Horse
Fantail
Filly
Foal
Gelding
Gotch-ear
Gut Twister
Hammerhead
Hay Burner
Indian Digger
Jughead
Killer
Knothead
Man Killer

Mare
Mount
Pony
Pinto
Plug
Roper

Saddler
Shavetail
Stallion
Stud
Usin' Horse
Wringtail

I Like Horses!

Yup, I like horses. Fact is that next to a pretty gal I'd rather have me a horse any day. And please don't call a horse dumb as I've seen lots of horses just as smart as a lot of us folks.

It seems that horses got their start as far back as fifty or sixty million years ago, or as some say even a hundred and sixty million years when dinosaurs were ruling the roost. It's said that the earliest horse was called the "dawn" horse having five toes on both front and hind feet. But as time went on — a few years, er I mean a few million years, they seem to have lost a couple of toes from each foot. And believe it or not, each toe had its own hoof and the body was covered with fur instead of hair.

By the way, how would you like to have a horsehide coat covered with fur instead of hair? Seems it would have been just as good as if made from a saber-toothed tiger or even from a good old raccoon same as Ma used to have. After we hit the ranch Ma never had a need to wear the coat and it hung on a hook until it was near eaten up by moths.

Brother Twitt and I slept in the attic having no heat other than from the tin stovepipe that ran up through the roof. We made our bed on the floor so we could curl up around the pipe. For bed covers we had about everything from a buffalo robe to a couple of horse blankets, quilts, gunnysacks and finally Ma give in and we added the old raccoon coat to our pile of quilts.

It wasn't long however, 'til Twitt and I took turns wearin' the coat as we climbed down the ladder and out to the log portion of the house where the kitchen stove and eatin' table was. But it did give Twitt and me the honor of being the only ones at the breakfast table wearing a dinner jacket, or in this case, guess it would be a breakfast jacket.

Let's see now, where was I? Oh yes, I was talking about the little horses with a hoof on each of the original five toes and later on only three toes on each foot. I can't help but wonder at the racket the little fellers must have made with from twelve to twenty hoofs banging and rattling against each other. Must have sounded like a set of castanets or maybe more like the bones we used to rattle in the old days. I'll bet a four dollar dog that the most of the readers of this book don't even know what "rattlin' the bones" meant, do you?

Well, I'll tell yuh what the "bones" were and looked like. As the name would imply they may have been made out of bones, but those we had were made out of hard wood. The drier the better. All it took was four pieces of hardwood about eight inches long, an inch wide and a half inch or so thick before being whittled down to having a bend as per the drawing.

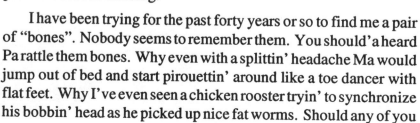

Held between the fingers and the fleshy inside of the thumb we could, with an up and down and sidewise shakin' of our hands, make a loud rattlin' noise guaranteed to start a person's feet to dancing.

I have been trying for the past forty years or so to find me a pair of "bones". Nobody seems to remember them. You should'a heard Pa rattle them bones. Why even with a splittin' headache Ma would jump out of bed and start pirouettin' around like a toe dancer with flat feet. Why I've even seen a chicken rooster tryin' to synchronize his bobbin' head as he picked up nice fat worms. Should any of you readers know where I can get a set of "bones", I shore would be most grateful.

So much for the bones so maybe I better get back to my little horses.

Let's talk about those archaeologist fellers. They do a lot of diggin' and pryin' around for anything old. And should they find even a tiny piece of bone from the top of a man's head they will jump on it like a chicken hawk on a covey of quail. When they get their teeth into such a nice juicy morsel, yuh can't pry them loose with a crowbar. Give 'em a little piece of a tooth and they will swear to High Heaven that the feller as used to wear the tooth was how old, how tall, what he had for breakfast and one feller claimed that the little horses used to be meat eaters! Well, everybody to his own taste, said the old woman as she kissed the cow.

And did yuh ever notice that when those archaeologist fellers dig up something they are not sure what it might be, they make up a big sounding name such as you can't even spell let alone pronounce.

Here is a good example of some names they thought up for some bones they thought might be prehistoric little horses: *Eohippus, Mesphippus, Michippus, Merychipus, Pliohippus, Equus.* Why those long hair fellers themselves can't even pronounce the words let alone know if they found the remains of a kangaroo or a woodpecker. Most of them big names up above sound more like hippopotamus than they do a woodpecker.

I don't remember where it was, but someone is said to have found a bone pile of a couple thousand horse skeletons. This makes a man wonder if the natives around there ate a lot of horse meat or whether a calamity of some sort hit that would account for that many skeletons in one pile. However, I can't see why horse meat shouldn't be just as good eating as any other meat. We might be surprised to know how much horse meat is sold over our meat counters even today.

I aimed to tell you about how many horses there now are in our states as well as in the world. I find it almost impossible to come up with a reliable figure. At one time I had a figure of from ten to twelve million here in the states. That gave me quite a little leeway until I heard that there are probably 150,000,000 world wide. So it looks as though I will have to shake the bushes to come up with more accurate figures. And you know I'm not too strong on evolution and it's hard for me to believe that a little dog size animal could end up as a 2,000 pound draft horse.

So let's say that the horse has been around for maybe 50,000,000 or even 165,000,000 years. But let's remember that during most of this time us human folks hadn't appeared on the scene until the coming of the stone age. I can't see any reason why I should

Serves yuh right! Hope yuh break yore damn jaw!

continue to hash up a lot of these outlandish figures as they are only guesses at best. But it seems that man first tamed wild horses on the steppes of Southwestern Europe or Asia, which would make it a couple of thousand years before Christ. These stone age fellers first hunted the horse for food, milk and hides. In later years the barbarian nomads used highly trained horses on the field of battle to haul chariots, etc.

Then with the coming of the Christian era, hand weapons such as the bow and arrow and the javelin or spear came into use. These weapons pretty much did away with the use of the chariot. Horses called chargers were used to carry the fighters into battle. At first these fighters used light and fast horses. But as time progressed, heavier horses were used as the horses were loaded down with heavy armor - as well as the rider himself who was at times completely enclosed in tin or metal armor. These loads required the largest and strongest of horses to carry the heavy load.

This, in turn, developed into the mounted cavalry such as was used by General Custer, Teddy Roosevelt and others with varying success. Then came the modern war machine such as the cannon and in rapid succession guns, tanks, planes, bombs, rockets and on into proposed star wars. Does this mean that we must say adieu to the noble steed that served us so well for the past few thousand years? Not by a jugfull we don't.

No, in fact they have just come into their own. From hard and dangerous work they are now the pampered pets of thousands. They are proudly ridden by kings and queens and are top billing when it comes to parades, circus performers, horse races, fox hunting, the Kings Royal Horse Artillery, big game hunting, hauling beer wagons, riding the range and finally to the good old rodeo where they can really let off steam. At one time in my memory we used to trade a couple of dogs for an Indian digger pony.

YUP, I SHORE LIKE HORSES!

About as busy as a hibernatin' bear.

BREEDS OF LIGHT HORSES, PONIES, DRAFT HORSES & ASSES

LIGHT HORSES AND PONIES

Breed	Origin	Color
American Buckskin	United States	Buckskin, red, dun, gruella.
American Gotland Horse	Gotland, Sweden	Bay, brown, black, dun, chestnut, palomino, roan and some leopard and blanket markings.
American Mustang	North Africa[1]	Any color.
American Paint Horse	United States	White, plus any other color. Must be a recognizable paint.
American Saddle Horse	United States - (Fayette County, KY)	Bay, brown, chestnut, gray or black. Gaudy white markings are frowned upon.
American Walking Pony	United States (Macon, Georgia, 1968)	No color stipulation. A cross between Welsh Pony and Tennessee Walking Horse; hence the colors of both parents' breeds occur.
American White	United States[2]	Snow white hair, pink skin, light blue, dark blue (near black), brown or hazel eyes.
American Cream (American Albino)[3]	United States - (Washington & Oregon)	Pale cream.
Andalusian	Spain	White and bay.
Appaloosa	United States[4]	Variable, but usually white over the loin and hips, with dark round or egg-shaped spots thereon

Breed	Origin	Color
Arabian	Arabia	Bay, gray and chestnut with an occasional white or black. White marks on the head and legs are common. Skin is always dark.
Chickasaw	United States[5]	Bay, black, chestnut, gray, roan, sorrel & palomino.
Cleveland Bay	Yorkshire, England (Cleveland District)	Always solid bay with black legs.
Connemara Pony	Ireland's West Coast	Gray, black, bay, brown, dun, cream with occasional roans and chestnuts.
Galiceno	Balicia, Spain	Solid colors prevail. Bay, black, chestnut (sorrel), dun (buckskin), gray brown and palomino are most common.
Hackney	England[6]	Chestnut, bay and brown are most common colors although roans and blacks are seen. White marks are common and desired.
Hungarian Horse	Hungary	All colors, either solid or broken.
Lipizzan	Lipizza, Yugoslavia	White, but Lipizzan foals are born dark (brown or gray) then turn white at 4 to 6 years of age. About one in 600 remain black or brown throughout life, which is considered good luck.
Missouri Fox Trotting Horse	United States (Ozark & Arkansas hills)	Sorrels predominate but any color is accepted.

(LIGHT HORSES AND PONIES . . . Continued)

Breed	Origin	Color
Morgan	United States	Bay, brown, black and chestnut. Extensive white markings are uncommon.
Morocco Spotted Horse	United States	Spotted. Secondary color white — which must comprise not less than 10%, not including legs or white on the face.
National Appaloosa Pony	United States Rochester, Indiana	All colors, with the following most popular: leopard, blanket type, snowflake or roan.
Palomino	United States (Spanish extraction)	Golden (the color of a newly minted gold coin or three shades lighter or darker) with a light colored mane and tail (white, silver or ivory with not more than 15% dark or chestnut hair in either). White markings on face or below the knees are acceptable.
Paso Fino	Peru, Puerto Rico, Cuba and Columbia	Any color although solid colors are preferred.
Peruvian Paso	Peru	Any color although solid colors are preferred.
Pinto	United States (Spanish extraction)	Preferably half color or colors and half white, with many spots well placed. The two distinct pattern markings are Overo and Tobiano.
Pony of the Americas	United States (Mason City, Iowa)	Similar to Appaloosa, white over the loin and hips with dark round or egg-shaped spots.

Breed	Origin	Color
Quarter Horse	United States	Chestnut, sorrel, bay and dun are most common, although they may be palomino, black, brown, roan or copper colored.
Shetland Pony	Shetland Isles	All colors, either solid or broken.
Spanish Barb	United States[7]	All colors. Dun, gruella, sorrel and roan are the most common. Most animals are solid color.
Spanish Mustang	United States[8]	They run the gamut of equine colors, including all the solid colors and all the broken colors.
Standardbred	United States	Bay, brown, chestnut and black are most common, but grays, roans and duns are found.
Tennessee Walking Horse	United States (Tennessee Middle Basin)	Sorrel, chestnut, black, roan, white, bay, brown, gray and golden. White markings on the face and legs are common.
Thoroughbred	England	Bay, brown, chestnut and black; less frequently roan and gray. White markings on the face and legs are common.
Welsh Pony	Wales	Any color except piebald and skewbald. Gaudy white markings are not popular.
Ysabella[9]	United States[10]	Gold, white or chestnut with flaxen, silver or white mane and tail.

DRAFT HORSES

Breed	Origin	Color
American Cream Horse	United States	Cream with white mane and tail and pink skin. Some white markings.
Belgian	Belgium	Bay, chestnut and roan are most common, but browns, grays and blacks are occasionally seen. Many Belgians have a flazen mane and tail and a white blazed face.
Clydesdale	Scotland (Along the River Clyde)	Bay and brown with white markings are most com mon, but blacks, grays, chestnuts and roans are occasionally seen.
Percheron	France (Dist. of La Perche)	Mostly black or gray, but bays, browns, chestnuts and roans are seen.
Shire	England[11]	Common colors are bay, brown and black with white markings, although grays, chestnuts and roans are occasionally seen.
Suffolk	England (East. County of Suffolk)	Chestnut only.

ASSES

Breed	Origin	Color
Jacks and Jennets	Domesticated in Egypt	Black with white nose; red, gray
Donkeys & Miniature	Sardinia and Sicily	Mouse color to almost black.

FOOTNOTES:

1. North African Barbary Coast, thence taken to Spain by the conquering Moors; propagated in Andalusia; thence brought to America by the Conquistadores. American Mustang Assoc. formed in 1962.
2. White Horse Ranch in Naper, Nebraska.
3. Both American White and American Cream are registered by the Am. Albino Assoc. in Crabtree, Oregon.
4. Primarily in Oregon, Washington and Idaho from animals originating in Fergana, Central Asia.
5. Developed by Chickasaw Indians of Tennessee, North Carolina and Oklahoma from horses of Spanish extraction.
6. Eastern Coast of England in Norfolk and adjoining counties.
7. Descended from Barb-Andalusian horse brought to America by the Spaniards in the 1500's and 1600's.
8. Beginning about 1925, Robert E. Brislawn, Sr. began gathering them on his ranch at Oshoto, Wyoming.
9. Named after Queen Isabella of Spain.
10. First bred at Mckinzie Rancho, Williamsport Indiana. Foundation animals were American Saddlers.
11. Primarily in the East Central counties of Lincolnshire and Cambridgeshire.

By permission of the publisher. Copyright © 1977 by A. S. Barnes & Company. Inc. *The Complete Encyclopedia of Horses* by M. E. Ensminger

* * * * *

He was always packin' one of them "brings 'em up close" things.

How to Tell the Age of Horses

Age is, of course, an important factor in the value of livestock. A good judge of horses should be able to estimate their age fairly accurately from a colt to 15 years. After sixteen or seventeen years it is much more difficult to tell with any degree of accuracy.

A horse fed on hard dry feed is likely to have teeth that show more wear than those of a horse fed on succulent feed. A further indication of age is when hairs appear around the temples, the eyes, nostrils and elsewhere. The sides of the face are more depressed and the cavities above the eyes more hollowed out than in middle aged horses. The backbone is prominent and is often swayed.

When a colt is foaled, it has no teeth showing. The first four front teeth in both upper and lower jaws are called incisors. In two to four days the first or middle pair of teeth will appear. The second or intermediate pair in from four to six weeks, and the third or lateral in from nine to twelve months of age. The age of a horse under two and a half years can usually be figured pretty close by the size and general appearance of the animal. Usually a colt will have a complete set of incisors (called milk teeth) when one year of age. These so called milk teeth will usually be retained until the colt is about two-and-one-half to three years old at which time they will start being replaced by permanent incisors.

A mature male horse has 40 teeth - twenty-four molars or grinders, twelve incisors or front teeth, and four tusks or pointed teeth. Mature mares have thirty-six teeth, and very rarely have any tusk teeth.

Age of Horses
(as shown by the teeth)

Courtesy: Bill Weddle — Tucson, Arizona

 *One Year*

 *Three Years*

 *Five Years*

 *Seven Years*

 *Nine Years*

 *Eleven Years*

 *Thirteen Years*

 *Fifteen Years*

 *Seventeen Years*

 *Nineteen Years*

A Cow Puncher and his Saddle

Back quite a few years ago cattle were big business. Most of the ranch owners had wives, but there were near thousands of punchers not so lucky. But they all did have themselves a saddle. A saddle was a cow puncher's life blood. It not only earned him a living, and furnished his transportation (if he could find a hoss to cinch it down on) but it would serve as a pillow to soften mother earth as he slept beneath the stars.

It was always with him. Should you see a puncher waiting around a stage stop or a depot, carrying a gunnysack, you didn't have to guess what was in it. You knew that it held his saddle along with a clean, though much wrinkled, Sunday shirt and a handful of personal items. The gunnysack was his only home.

His saddle was always the best he could afford and would cost about two or three months' wages. Of course, a little stamping or a bit of carving on it didn't do any harm when it came to charming the gals (very scarce). With his two-inch boot heels and jingling spurs which he wore when he "lit out to the town hole" it shore made for a lot of flashiarity which a cowboy always craved.

Yuh could probably borrow a man's iron should you have something to shoot, and for a real good reason yuh might borrow his hoss, but don't insult him by asking to borrow his saddle. Oh no, as to him it's part of him and near sacred. Brother Ernie was such a breed. In all the years we lived on the Diamond N, not once did I ever step into his saddle. Nor while still a button did I ever climb up the side of his big buckskin hoss, Panther. Times innumerable he would ask me to put his Panther hoss on a pin up on the hillside back of the snow fence just above a 300' cattle shed dug into the hillside. Why, he wouldn't even let me ride him up the hill, which was just as well, 'cause Panther wasn't overly partial to lettin' a kid like me shinny up his laig to get on him bareback.

But to get back to the saddles. I have to grin when I read about how to buy a new saddle nowadays. One feller says to take pieces of cardboard or something and shape four or five of the pieces to fit the shape of the hoss' back from the withers back about two feet. Then all yuh got to do is take the hoss in the back door, if yuh can, or give the saddle maker the four pieces and he will make yuh a saddle guaranteed to exactly fit yore hoss.

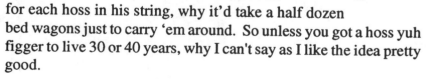

Sounds purty good, but the hell of it is if yore hoss should accidently step into a badger hole an' yuh had to shoot him, then yuh would be up the creek with a $2,000 saddle and no hoss with a back to fit it. Gosh, if a feller had to have a saddle like that for each hoss in his string, why it'd take a half dozen bed wagons just to carry 'em around. So unless you got a hoss yuh figger to live 30 or 40 years, why I can't say as I like the idea pretty good.

The way we used to do it was to get our saddles from first-class outfits like Al Furstnow or Miles City Saddlery of Miles City, Montana. Now them fellers knew how to make saddles. We'd mostly buy what they had made up but should we want 'em a little different like maybe weight, swell, riggin' an' such, why we could depend on a first-rate saddle fittin' for most average hoss backs. A good saddle maker knows how to average out a saddle be it one with high withers or for flatter hosses. We could mostly step up on the average hoss without fastenin' the cinch.

I suspect saddles are made pretty near as good nowadays, but they shore ain't none better than we had. Shore, I know about rodeo gear and those postage stamp kind which I call pavement saddles maybe to ride down the lane to get the mail. I'm talkin' about stock saddles that we had in the old days. I shore wish I could run across my old saddle. It's got "Frosty" scratched under the flap.

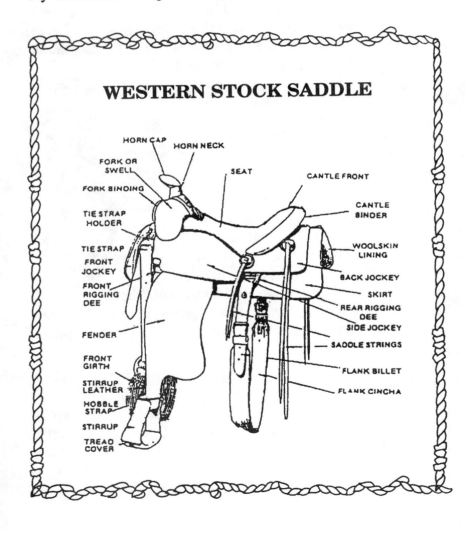

WESTERN STOCK SADDLE

HORN CAP
HORN NECK
FORK OR SWELL
SEAT
CANTLE FRONT
FORK BINDING
CANTLE BINDER
TIE STRAP HOLDER
WOOLSKIN LINING
TIE STRAP
FRONT JOCKEY
BACK JOCKEY
FRONT RIGGING DEE
SKIRT
REAR RIGGING DEE
SIDE JOCKEY
FENDER
SADDLE STRINGS
FRONT GIRTH
FLANK BILLET
STIRRUP LEATHER
FLANK CINCHA
HOBBLE STRAP
STIRRUP
TREAD COVER

Cattle Rustling Terms

Cattle rustling was a serious matter and a wide variety of terms were developed to describe those who participated in this activity.

Brand artist
Brand blotter
Brand worker
Careless with his
    brandin' iron
Ear carver
He's a rope and ring man
His cows have twins
His calves don't suck
    the right cows

Rawhide burner
He rides with an extra
    cinch ring
Sleepering
Slow brander
Sticky roper
Uses a long rope
Wet brander
Works ahead of
    the roundup

Cattle and Cattle Brands

Startin' back in about 1903 in all the years of cattle ranching we never did have what is known as a milk cow as we now know them. When calves started coming in early spring, Pa would keep his eye on a cow having a big bag that could be expected to give a lot of milk. After the new calf had sucked a few days we would put the cow in a small pasture with a shed for stormy weather. We mostly ran Herefords which are not supposed to be very good milk cows, so we would pick some off-breed critter. None of us would eat young calves so we would usually trade them to the Indians for a pair of moccasins, or by throwin' in a small dog or two we might even get an Indian digger (a poor excuse of a horse).

I dug up some figures called Statistics that shows that in the United States alone there are around 105,000,000 cows of which 11,000,000 are milk cows. It doesn't seem worthwhile to list all of the breeds of cattle worldwide, so I have shown only those in the United States. I hope I am fairly close as there are some borderline breeds I may have omitted.

Should yuh still might want to dig further why go on down to the library. You'll be surprised at all of the books they got. Why yuh can find out about near everything yuh can think of, and even some things yuh probably shouldn't even know about.

The Dry Season

In nineteen thirty-one, on May the twenty-third,
We cut out all the yearlins' — 300 in a herd.
It was shortly after breakfast, the men were all outside,
Tom says, saddle up your pony, boys, we're goin' to take a ride.

The grass is gettin' greener — we're goin' to make a change,
We're a goin' to take these yearlins' up to the summer range.
We'll take 'em up the mountain, where there's water, feed an' shade,
That's the very finest country the good Lord ever made.

We'd had 'em up the mountain about a month or so,
When the grass was turnin' brown, an' the springs was runnin' low.
We'll clean out all the springs, an' that might be of some use,
The yearlin's won't make canners, with their bawlin' and abuse.

A pushin' back his hat, an' moppin' off his head,
Pointin' to a critter, these words he grimly said.
Just look there at old Ronie, he's gant an' dry as hell,
His neck has shrunk so small that he's even lost his bell.

Cattle all a bawlin', wrinkles in their hide,
Magpies have all left us, an' the cottontails have died.
An' with this hot wind blowin' — it' lookin' pretty blue
We just gotta move those yearlins', that's all there's left to do.

by Frosty Potter

BREEDS OF CATTLE IN UNITED STATES

Angus	Charolaise	Hereford	Polled Shorthorn
Barzona	Chianina	Holstein	Red Angus
Beef Frieslan	Devon	Jersey	Red Polled
Braford	Dairy Shorthorn	Limousin	Maine-Anjou
Brahama	Duel Purpose	Lincoln Red	Milking Shorthorn
Brangus	Gelvbieh	Longhorns	Simmental
Beefmaster	Gry Sussex	Murray Grey	Scotch Highland
Brown Swiss	Galloway	Ndama	Zebu
Charbray	Gurnsey	Polled Herefords	

Cattle Brands and How to Read Them

Cattle brands have been kickin' around for the better part of four or five thousand years. This is easily proven as geologists and anthropologists and others have found literally thousands of paintings and carvings in ancient caves and tombs showing old mossy-horn bulls with brands. Evidently such brands were in use as much as two thousand years before Christ.

As near as I can find, brands were first used in our country about the year 1522. These early brands were probably found on cattle brought over from Spain about that time. Yet, in spite of this early age, cattle brands were not used extensively in our part of the country until around 1775, and it wasn't until a hundred years later that they came into big use. History has it that Cortez was the first to use a brand in North America. His brand was three Christian crosses. † † †

Charlie Goodnight and John Chisholm were among the first of the big cattle moguls to use "trail brands" on their big drives to northern ranges so as to identify their own stock from other drives on the trails.

The lowly cattle brand can be the answer as a means of identification other than to use numbers, etc. Brands are easily remembered, whereas names, letters, and such are easily forgotten.

To prove my point I will list a few cattle brands that even you, who never owned a cow critter, are probably familiar with. Do you know who owns the Seven Up ᴜᴘ, Ten in Texas ✕ l T, Damned Hard Settin' Ɒ-ꞓ, Rocking Chair ⊔, Wine Glass ⸆, or the Elkhorn ⪤ ? Some of them are probably still in business today.

A brand on a critter denotes ownership in which a man can take pride. In fact, his brand is often far better known than the owner himself. A brand usually follows the ranch, not an individual. Believe me, a man who owns a cattle brand is prouder of his brand than he is of his wife with the kids thrown in. His brand is his outfit, everything he owns, and, believe me, he will fight at the drop of a hat for everything it represents.

Should his brand be Rafter K ⟨K, inquiries regarding his stock would probably be "Isn't that lineback a Rafter K?", instead of "Ain't that John Peterson's lineback?"

So what I am trying to tell you is, a brand isn't just to put on your cattle, it serves to identify you about like a credit card does, or the fact that you belong to the Elk's Club.

I haven't lived on a cattle ranch for the past 50 or so years, yet my brand, the Diamond N, appears on both sides of my cars, on my business cards, implanted in my fresh cement sidewalk, on my driveway, my mailbox, my belt buckle, and would appear on my hot air balloon - if I owned one.

I have even gone one step further in having adopted the nickname "Frosty" since I was 4 or 5 years old. My brand and my nickname have almost taken over in that a large part of my mail is addressed "Frosty", my check blanks show "Frosty" and even my checks are signed with the single word "Frosty". Yup, it's taken me a long time to tell you what I have told you above, which is that you should get yourself a brand. Make it part of your family tree.

So far I have only talked about brands that are burned into a critter's hide. There are other means used to help an owner identify his stock. Wattles, dewlaps, jug handles and the wide use of ear crops. These are all made by cutting into the hide of the critter.

There are a number of ways a critter's ear can be marked by actually whittlin' off portions of the ear. I have seen a picture showing over a hundred different ways of carving ears. The reason for ear crops bein' so popular is that if a critter is branded on its side, the brand can only be read from that side. An ear crop can, of course, be seen from the rear, front or sidewise as the cattle are moving.

In the early days it was a common practice for a would-be rancher to get a start in the business by altering ear crops. This was rather ticklish business as yuh can't fool a calf's mother — she knows her own offspring.

Now altering brands is a horse of a different color. It's called rustling and I expect that there has been a couple thousand books written about this subject alone. It was, and still is, bad business to get caught at, as should yuh get caught in the act yuh could depend on bein' strung up on the nearest tree which snaps yore neck right pronto (usually at the first try). Of course, when yuh get hung from a tree, yuh don't get the benefits of a readin' or even nobody takes off his hat. Should a travelin' preacher happen along you can depend his diagnosis would most usually be "died of throat trouble".

Rustlin' was really a prime way to get a start in the cattle business. Should yuh have an artistic bent, yuh could figure it out with a little change here and a little change there and you could probably get by so as the brand would look different. In fact, I have read that there are 77 ways a brand can be changed, so it gives yuh quite a large variety of ways to build up yore herd should yuh want to try yore luck. Like I said, "a cow knows her calf" same as a calf knows her mother. In fact, should a rancher's ear cropped calf start suckin' a cow with an off brand, the feller who changed the brand had better head for Mexico or some other far away place.

Yuh know, sometimes I sort of envy the young folks. But when I think of the life we lived in those days, then I'm pretty sure I don't. I am sure that you folks who have grandpas, or maybe I should say great-grandpas, who used to own cattle ranches have heard him tell more than once how he got started in the cow business.

Has he told you how he lived maybe 40 miles from the nearest settlement having a couple of saloons and a scattering of other buildings, including a hotel and "another kind of hotel down the road-a-ways"? How he would stock up with a couple of snorts at the bar, get a sack of flour, likewise of sugar, some java, a five-pound box of raisins, and likely a five-gallon can of kerosene, a bottle of liniment, a bottle of sasparilla, a can of axle grease and a couple slabs of sowbelly. By the time he loaded his stuff on the ranch wagon, got hitched up and drove the 40 miles home, it would be plumb dark.

Yup, give the old boy a chance to talk with somebody like you to listen to him and he'll usually come up with some pretty hairy tales. Now I'm not about to say that I was with my grandpappy when he got his start, but I'm pretty near shore it started about like a page I am going to write later in this book. I'll call it *How Grandpa Got His Start.*

But first I promised to tell yuh about cattle brands and I still aim to do it. Cattle brands is a big subject and it would take a long time to cover everything you might want to know. A feller has to be near an artist

to draw pictures of brands and such, so instead of me tryin' to do it I am just going to include some pictures and it will give you an idea of how to read brands.

P. S. Should any of you readers decide to produce such a brand and nickname moniker, be sure to cut me in to the tune of about 51% of the gross intake. I'll be waitin' to hear from you . . .

Reading Brands

Lazy U Cross

Rocking Chair

L U Bar

PEG

H Hanging H

Maltese Cross

J P

F Running N

Backward E Two Bar

Turkey Track

Double Milliron

O Bar Lazy S

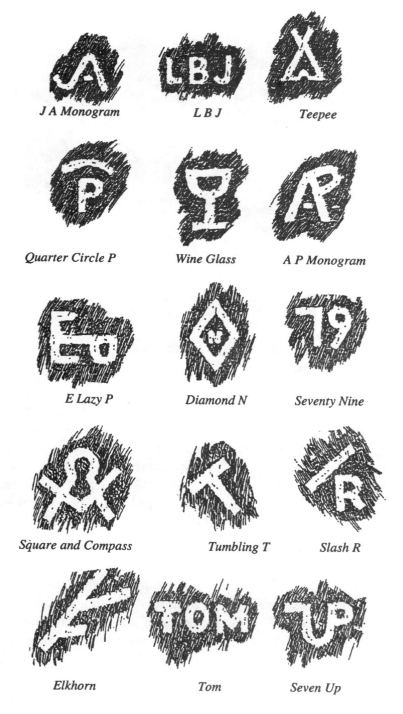

J A Monogram   L B J   Teepee

Quarter Circle P   Wine Glass   A P Monogram

E Lazy P   Diamond N   Seventy Nine

Square and Compass   Tumbling T   Slash R

Elkhorn   Tom   Seven Up

The Potter Family

A first Potter to come to the United States was in 1634. Our blood line is unbroken up to my great grandsons. I wanted to tell you least you might think I am a half breed of sorts.

Our family genealogy records go back at least to 1634 when Robert Potter and son Anthony came to this country and settled in Lynn, Massachusetts. Should you be interested in our genealogy I can tell you that Pa (Henry W. Potter) was born in North Conway, New Hampshire on November 17, 1855. He later moved, along with other Potters, to Iowa where he married Viola Libby who lived only two years after giving birth to their only child, Mable.

In due time Pa moved to Howard County in Iowa, and married Cora Louise Pooler. Together they had a big family, including me! While Pa's family was growing up, the Chicago Milwaukee Railway Company decided to build a railroad through the area and needed right of way. Pa's father, Lemual Potter 2nd, who lived on the land they wanted, agreed to give the company right of way if they would name the town Elma after one of Pa's sisters. That little town of Elma with a population of 714 still does business as usual.

Pa Buys the Diamond N Ranch

My older brothers were getting to be full grown and as Pa had been out to North Dakota one time he figured he would like to own a cattle ranch. So he bought the Diamond N Ranch which was located south of Mandan, North Dakota near the Cannonball River and the Sioux Indian Reservation.

In Iowa he sold his farm and rented a railway boxcar in which he loaded some furniture, horses, wagons and all such. It seems that one man (Pa) could ride free in the boxcar to take care of things, so he bought a ticket for Ernie and they were all set. But brothers Burt and Lynn (Curly), wanting to save train fare, built a wooden box big enough to get into. Now to save them from gettin' stuck in there, they made it with the cover hinging inward instead of upward. The idea being that if the brakeman came along to check things, they would get in the box and be able to get out again should other stuff be piled on top.

Pa and the boys had a little kerosene lantern stove over which they could cook. When the slow freight train would stop for coal or water, Pa and the boys would gather whatever vegetables as they could find along the tracks, and Pa did admit to havin' appropriated a few chickens that were feeding dangerously close to the track.

Ma, sister Myrtle, Ray and us three small kids came on the passenger train to Bismarck, and we soon had wagons loaded with all kinds of stuff. Then we had to ferry across the Missouri River between Bismarck and Mandan.

As this was before there were bridges across the Big Muddy (Missouri River), the only way to get across was to ride the ancient old ferryboat. Of course, during the winter when the river froze over, we could drive across on the ice. So if you wanted to go by train from Chicago to the West Coast, it was necessary to leave the train in Bismarck and ride the ferry across the river - or wait until

Laying tracks on the Missouri River ice.

the river froze over with as much as four to six feet of ice and again mount the train in Mandan about six miles west.

One year when the river was said to have frozen near to the bottom, the railroad company had actually laid their track on the ice. Been looking for a picture for the past month and finally found it. Needless to say, I am disappointed to find that the picture is not an actual photograph. However, having lived within 40 miles of this event and heard talk of it, I am fully satisfied it is the truth. In fact a few years later one of my brothers helped build the bridge across the Big Muddy.

Now Pa wasn't' the kind of feller who liked to be told what to do. When everything was loaded aboard the ferry and the ferry man decided to eat his lunch first, Pa didn't want to just sit there while he was eatin', so he tells him off in fourteen languages — which Pa could handle without missin' a word. We finally got to Mandan an' started down the trail past where General George Armstrong Custer took off to fight the Battle of the Little Big Horn in Montana where he an' his whole outfit was killed — to the last man.

We angled west a mite and hit what was left of the old Deadwood Stage line that ran near our Diamond N Ranch headquarters. A few Rooshuns had already started homesteadin' on farm land south of Mandan down about 30 miles where it dropped off to nothing but sagebrush, cactus and rattlesnakes.

We dropped down into the basin, crossed a couple of small creeks, rounded a bend in the trail and there she was, about as purty a spread as you would want to see. Right at the crotch where three wooded coulees came together, there were a few scattered huge oak trees, cherry and plum trees, blackhaws, bullberries and brush. The creeks and birds were singing their own brand of music with at least ten birds to a tree. Yup, we shore figured we was about to live in Heaven itself!

Our ranch was at the foot of the drop off where three spring fed creeks meandered across the basin or Dogtooth River and eventually into the Cannonball and Missouri River. These small springs originated at the base of the drop-off and formed what we called the "alkali beds". These beds were about the consistency and color of plaster, with bunch grass scattered throughout. These so called alkali runs were over a mile long and up to 200 feet wide. The whole area consisted of smaller beds from two feet wide up to ten or twenty feet wide. A small bed three feet in diameter was mostly round and would appear as if pressure had caused it to build up, about the consistency of mud. A pole could be pushed down ten feet or more without hitting bottom.

One of the runs, as they were called, was two or three hundred feet wide and seldom was an animal able to cross without getting bogged down. At times an area ten or twenty feet wide and covered with grass had the appearance of being safe to walk on. However, if we stood in the middle of it and jumped up and down, the entire island would bob up and down as much as six inches. Only an experienced horse would attempt to cross these runs.

Strange as it may seem, we had an Eastern bred horse named "Darky" who could cross the runs with no trouble. It was dangerous to cross with most horses cause if they hit a soft spot and sank up to their belly they would start to paw with their front feet and the rider could be pawed under. Forty or fifty years later when I visited the old ranch I could scarcely believe that the beds and runs had totally dried up. When I was around ten years old, it had been my job to "ride the runs" to see if there were any livestock bogged down.

Before the homesteaders started moving in, we had a chunk of free government graze land of twenty or twenty-five square miles. Most of this area was covered with buffalo grass known for its fattening quality. This grass was too short to mow for hay, but the grass could cure itself and was prime winter feed for cattle if it was not covered with snow. Unlike horses, cattle can't dig through the snow.

Haying was a big job as we had to cut and stack at least 400 loads of hay for our livestock. Pa and the four older boys and usually a man or two worked all summer long to cut the hay, haul it a mile or two and stack it near the ranch headquarters so as to be available during the rough winter weather.

Hell's fire, here I am with 400 loads of hay already in stacks and we haven't even moved in yet.

Well, here goes . . . .

The ranch house was a frame building made of 2 x 4 studs covered with rough siding, a single thickness of tar paper and topped off with drop siding. The single room was perhaps not more than 24 x 40 feet in size.

Pa and Ma slept behind a blanket strung across one corner of the house and sister Myrtle behind a horse blanket across another corner. Baby Max slept in a plank wood feed box from a horse stall. Ernie and Ray slept in the attic on some boards laid across the ceiling joists. When the lady mail carrier would get stuck in a blizzard and spend the night with us, she would sleep on a couple of boards in the attic too. So help me Hannah, I can't remember where brother Harry (Twitt) and I slept. Probably on the floor with a buffalo robe around us.

Burt (Pete) and Lynn (Curly) slept in an old bunkhouse with only a lantern for heat. It is now hard to believe that they could sleep in that bunkhouse when below zero, even 40 below. They would crawl into bed fully dressed except for their boots and come morning they would jump out of bed, grab their boots and run the 100 yards to the house in their Rockford socks. This arrangement went on for two years.

As our hay feeding area was not far from the house, cattle would hang around the barnyard until the ground would be covered with melting snow along with near inches of cow dung. We couldn't even step out the door without having our overshoes on, or we would catch hell from Ma.

We were just across the Cannonball River from the Sioux Standing Rock Indian Reservation.

In those days any person over 21 years of age could file on a 160 acre claim (or homestead) as they were called. Pa and Ma and my four older brothers and my sister, Mable, each filed for a homestead of 160 acres giving us seven quarter sections plus a school section that anybody could use as long as it was made use of such as for graze or cutting hay. So you can see we weren't pushed for hay land. Us three young'uns weren't old enough to file. The government retained a section in each township called a School Section, in case a school was ever built. Anyone making use of this school section could claim it if they made continuous use of it. As it was prime hay land, Pa of course laid claim to it year after year, thus we had plenty of prime hay land at our disposal.

The homestead laws said that a homesteader must build a house, or homestead shack as they were called, and live in it five years, or by living on it six months could commute by paying $125 and could own the property. So we built a shack on each of the claims. They ranged all the way from a sod or log hut to a frame shack. One could just dig a cave in the side of a hill and use stone or sod to fill in the front. My brother Burt says that his shack cost him $12.00.

A couple of boards with legs were nailed to the wall like a shelf for a bed, a homemade chair along with an apple box nailed on the wall for a cupboard, a knife, fork and spoon, a tin cup and a near empty coffee can and the homesteader was all set to marry himself a wife — that is, if he could find a wife — which was scarce to come by.

Some 350 head of "not too well bred" stock came with the ranch, but Pa immediately started building up the herd with top grade Hereford stock so that within a couple of years we had going on close to 1,000 head of top stuff.

I suspect I better tell you something about the ranch buildings themselves. There was a huge twelve stall barn with a lean-to for ridin' stuff. The barn was made out of heavy hand sawed planks from General Custer's headquarters about 15 miles away. The haymow above the barn had a hay lift so that many loads of hay could be stored against stormy weather.

Out back was a cow hospital where we kept sick or wounded animals or young calves, a buggy or wagon shed (we never did own a buggy) a lean-to blacksmith shop setting on the edge of the creek, and a small chicken coop. In the back of the barns we also had a holdin' corral with a 300 foot long cattle shed which was partly dug into the hill behind the barn. The back of the building was against the hillside and was made of eight foot poles set upright. The front and ends of the buildings were left open for ventilation. The roof

Hey Ma — did yuh bring all the kids?

was made of cross logs covered with brush with six or eight inches of hay on top of it.

We had a well eight feet deep as couldn't be pumped dry if pumped all day long. But the well was so close to the barn and corrals that drainage would seep into the well so that the water looked more like tea than it did drinking water. But whoever drank from the well claimed that it was the best water they had ever drunk. It's easy to see that they had good reason to remember it.

Ma would always cook for 10 or 12 people. Our family amounted to ten and then there were always friends and neighbors dropping in. Don't forget, our house was also the Post Office for Diamond, ND and served as a schoolhouse at certain times of the year.

For breakfast, Ma used an 18 inch skillet over the wood cook stove to fry her flapjacks. Batter consisted of flour, eggs, milk and salt. The eggs, milk and salt were stirred into the flour while it was still in the bag. This provided a "mixing bowl" of sorts. The skillet would hold 7 flapjacks and each would be given one at a time going around the table several times. No syrup was available in those days, so Ma would make bullberry sauce from berries available on bushes about six miles south of the ranch. Those berries were small, red and had a tiny pit in the center. Ma would boil the berries, strain them through a flour sack and then add a small amount of sugar. Then she would seal the sauce in two gallon glass jars. One jar was enough for a couple of breakfasts. Ma put up a couple hundred jars each summer, hopefully enough to get through the next winter.

Pa and Ma had a large garden which was located about a mile from the house, down where water was available from the well. We raised corn, cantaloupe, muskmelon, and potatoes. Most of the harvest was placed into the cellar which was not much more than a cave carved into the side of a hill located not too far from the house. The little kids had to go into the cellar frequently to take the sprouts off of the potatoes. The corn was not the good sweet corn

The old Diamond N Ranch house — 1903

we have nowadays. Instead it was about the same as what we now call field corn.

When we needed meat, Pa would kill a calf and let it hang for about three days. This would permit the meat to drain, cool and cure. After that Ma would put the meat up in jars. The meat would also freeze in the winter which would make it keep even longer.

We went to our own forty-miles-from-nowhere school. Pa and the older boys cleaned out an old dirt floor log bunkhouse and nailed together a couple of benches to set on. Then by appropriatin' an old wooden feed bin from the barn, we had the makin's of a desk we could all set around and write on. A yard or so of black tar paper nailed to a wall served as a blackboard to do our higher mathematics on.

I don't know where Pa got it, but we had a huge cast iron coal and wood burnin' stove with a scad of little isinglass windows on all four sides. Guess it would have burned better if us kids hadn't poked out some of the windows.

The school board furnished some McGuffy readers along with a half dozen spellin' books and a box of white pieces of chalk to write on the tar paper blackboard. It didn't take us long to find that by holdin' the chalk at the right angle to the blackboard it would squeak like all get out. The teacher soon found out that a short piece of chalk wouldn't squeak, so we ended up with a box of short pieces — of the teacher's making.

Pa had to furnish the school house as well as a teacher, who was my half-sister, Mable. Keeping the school warm was always a big problem. Pa didn't want to cut down the big oak trees in our coolies, so we tried mostly to use coal. Not the store bought kind, but from our own coal mine, if it could be called that.

Our coal mine was an eight to ten inch strip of what looked like coal in a seam runnin' crosswise of a cliff. All we had to do was take a team of horses and a small scoop shovel with handles on it and scrape off five or six feet of dirt to reach the coal. We could actually dig out chunks near half as big as our heads, but let them lay a few days and they would "slack" and crumble to nothing but glorified black dirt. Usually with a hot fire of burning wood, that old coal would just lay there and smolder even with one of us boys on hands and knees trying to blow up a draft.

So fifty degrees below outside usually meant not much above zero inside. This, of course, meant that we had to wear our long johns topped with a wool shirt or two, if we had two - which we usually didn't. On top of that we wore our heavy sheep-lined coats with big wool collars turned up, a stockin' cap or a cap with pull down ear flaps, a pair of heavy leather mittens with separate wool liners, and, of course, a heavy pair of wool pants for the boys and a dress of who-knew-what for the girls, and four-buckle overshoes to top the two or three pair of wool socks. It also helped to tuck our pant legs into the tops of our overshoes or even stuff some paper in our pant legs.

I near forgot to mention us kids who went to school. First there was me and brother Twitt. Max was too young to go to school. Then sister Mutt who was two years older than me. Then besides the above mentioned, there was the three pretty little Kellogg girls from down on the Cannonball River. Their Pa would drive them up the six miles when weather permitted.

Fred Port lived about six or eight miles over west and would ride his hoss every mornin'. Sometimes he was so damn cold we near had to pry him loose from his saddle. But never once did he stay all night, said his Pa would whale hell out of him if he didn't show up to prove that he wasn't stuck some place in a ten foot drift of snow.

After a couple of years Pa moved all of the school furniture such as the two benches and the feed box down to the Kellogg ranch. And Pa even gave Mister Kellogg a fresh piece of tar paper for the blackboard. Every Monday morning Pa or one of the boys would draw straws to see who would drive us kids in a bobsled down to the Kellogg ranch and then come and get us Friday if the weather was good enough. Otherwise we would stay with the Kellogg girls (or I should say the Kellogg family) for another week.

About then I believe it was that brother what's-his-name (I'd better not name him) and me and another feller, with the help of Charlie Rattlin' Tail, an Indian, stole quite a few of the unbranded Indian digger ponies.

One time we had about 75 or 80 on hand when we heard that the sheriff might make a call on us, so we beat him to the gun by shovin' them down near the Black Hills and sold them to the last cavalry in the United States (so it's said) at Fort something or other, I can't quite remember the name.

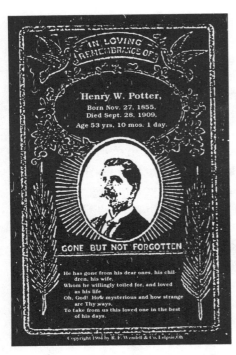

Pa Killed While Shipping Cattle

Every fall we would join with other ranchers to ship our beef cattle to the Union Stock Yards in Chicago. This would represent a train load of cattle that had to be taken care of while en route. Each rancher would provide a man or two to go along with his own shipment to feed and water his cattle.

Pa always took along one of my older brothers. 1909 was my year to go along but I was laid up with a bum leg and couldn't go. Pa decided to go alone. To provide sleeping accommodations the railroad company would usually arrange to have one or two cabooses, or a couple of times they had provided an old passenger coach.

A few days after Pa left, a railroad employee came riding in to tell us the bad news. He said the stock train had pulled onto a side track of the Union Stockyards to wait until daylight to unload the stock. Apparently an employee had carelessly left a switch open and a fast passenger train had crashed into the back of the cattle train killing a railway employee and all of the eight ranchers asleep in the two cabooses. A number of cattle in the cars ahead were also killed or crippled.

That was a sad day for the Diamond N. Brother Twitt and I were hunting prairie chicken when the railroad man gave Ma the bad news. Tom Edel, a ranch hand, had located us and without a waste of words said, "Hurry up and go home. Your Pa is killed."

After a few short years, my four older brothers started getting married and left the ranch. Without Pa the ranch gradually went downhill and Ma sold it in 1917, I believe it was.

As homesteaders continued to move in, cattle ranching was a thing of the past. All of the ranch buildings have been removed.

I have in recent years visited the site a couple of times and the only consolation I got was to see that a prairie dog colony now occupied the former site of our hay corral.

He saddled a cloud and rode to the great beyond.

How Grandpa Got His Start

Picture Grandpa settin' on his hoss...few dogies stand off lookin' at him...he sizes up the critters...takes himself a hard look up and down, sidewise, crosswise and slantwise...he slides down the side of his hoss...builds him a little no-smoke fire out of a weed or two and a few cow chips ...loosens his saddle girth 'nough to unfasten a little iron ring...puts the little iron ring in the fire...shakes out his twine...drops it over the neck of a calf...bunches together as many legs as he can grab...ties them together with piggin' string, neckerchief, or a sleeve torn out of his best Sunday shirt...slips a couple of green weeds through the now hot ring...and with a diabolical grin...does his art work for the day...rubs a handful of dirt over the hide picture he has just made so it will look kind of old...scuffs the little ring in the dirt to cool...stomps and waters out the little fire ...replaces the little ring on latigo strap...ties loose the one time maverick...coils his twine and hangs it on the saddle...then freezes...though it's 110° in the shade...of which there ain't any...stares at a puff of dust in front of him...hears a crack of thunder, which it ain't...trips over his spurs as he jumps to tighten his saddle girth ...climbs up the side of his hoss...clamps laigs under hoss's belly...buries his hocks in soft flesh...feels to see if his 30-30 is under his laig...his 45 rubbin' his thigh...pulls hat down tight with thong under his chin...takes a backward look...changes hoss's head from home to another direction ...keeps an eye out for badger holes...hits the breeze and wonders if his hoss can outrun the rabbit ahead...prays he can beat the bunny...and he does!!

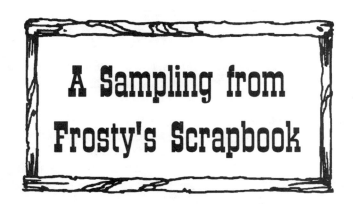

A Sampling from Frosty's Scrapbook

Cowboy Sayin's

"JUSTICE" FRONTIER STYLE

Cowboys used some colorful terms for frontier style "justice".

Bed him down
Bit the dust
Blow out his lamp
Buck out
Bushwhack
Curled him up

Downed him
Dry gulch
Hang up his hide
Land him in a shallow grave
Made wolf meat out o' him
Put a window in his skull

COWBOY TALK

Known for their taciturnity, cowboys nevertheless found plenty of words to describe those whom they felt talked too much!

Argurin' match
Chew the fat
Chew the cud
Cow talk
Coyotin' 'round the rim
Dallying his tongue
Diarrhea of the jawbone
Flannel mouth
Had some conversation fluid

Leaky mouth
Moccasin mail
More lip than a
    muley cow
Musta' got a dose of tongue oil
Pow wow
Talking talent
Too much tonsil varnish
Windies

Baseball, Football, or Rodeoin'?

You've heard me say at least a dozen times that a rodeo is the finest sport there is. But to test what other folks think, I am going to take you to a baseball game and see if you can work yourself into the high state of frenzy that the rodeo did. So here goes . . . .

BASEBALL

In the first place it seems to me that you have to do a lot of hard settin' hour after hour, maybe in the rain, or with the sun a beatin' down on your head, watchin' first one feller after another tryin' to hit a little ball that the pitcher - standin' on a little hill - keeps tossing at him. And even if the battin' feller does hit the little ball once in awhile, all he does is throw his club as far as he can (makin' folks duck from gettin' hit), and then run like hell to see if he can get over to first base before the ball gets there.

Usually they both get there about the same time. Then a big feller standin' there with a common suit of clothes on, has got to decide who got there first. Of course if the battin' feller had hit the little ball clear to the back fence, then he keeps runnin' like all get out to see if maybe he can get clear around the track and slide in on his belly before the ball comes a whizzin' in. I guess the feller with the leggins' on, called the catcher, is supposed to touch the runner with it and another big feller with a plain suit on yells "yere out". Then makes him go and set in the bull pen with the rest of the spares.

Of course, a runner only gets clear around the track every couple hours or so, but when he does, all hell breaks loose. Even the big feller with the plain suit turns a back somersault with a handspring or two, and all of the players jump on each others back and hug and kiss everybody in sight. And the folks up in the settin' seats. You'd ought to see them! They all jump to their feet scatterin' babies all over the floor as they yell and holler, wave flags and scream to high Heaven. As everybody is gettin' kissed, the poor hittin' feller tries to sneak away so he can go and hide in the little doghouse where the spares sit. And all of that fuss over one lousy score. Why when us kids used to play out back of the barn our scores might be maybe 45 to 86 at least. Course when I watch I don't care what the score is, I only have fun watchin' the players chasin' that little ball all over the corral pen.

Now let me wise you up to something you probably never noticed. The pitcher throws the ball. . . now watch the catcher. If the ball lands in the dirt, he will pick it up, make believe he is looking it over very careful, and then hand it to the umpire.

Now this is where the dirty work comes in. Mister Umpire will make us believe the ball is dirty or bruised and will slip it into one of the made to order oversize pockets of his coat and hand the catcher a brand new ball to throw out to the pitcher. Now you tell me how come the umpire has to keep so darn many of those just as good as new balls? It looks like a cooked up deal between the catcher and the umpire. Why, I've watched a ball boy carry pail after pail of new balls over to the umpire and no one says a word about it. And I've heard that for some games they use maybe two or three hundred balls. So is it any wonder that those umpires can afford to wear such nice blue suits all pressed up, and I'll bet that they all probably drive at least a Cadillac or even a Mercedes Benz. And I am pretty sure that one time I saw a big feller with a nice blue suit on get into a Rolls Royce!

And did you ever pay particular attention to those pitchin' fellers? Why they got so many tricks up their sleeve now days that the poor batters mostly just stand there swingin' their bat and so confused they don't know whether to take a swipe at the ball or duck so's not to get hit.

Course he only gets a few chances to try, and if he gets tired tryin' or they feel sorry for him the umpire will either let him go back to the doghouse or let him walk slow out to first base where he can rest up before tryin' to sneak around to home plate. I particularly like to watch when a batter hits the ball and it goes straight up in the air. The catcher jerks off his mask, throws it on the ground and staggers around like a migratin' bullfrog tryin' to keep his eye on the ball so's to catch it if he can. Why he doesn't even look to see where he's goin', and one time I seen him crash into the fence which flopped him ass-over-teakettle and he landed slap dab into the lap of a pretty gal who was settin' in a front seat. Nope, he didn't get hurt none, but made believe he was so he could get to set in her lap a little longer.

And did you ever notice when the catcher is squatted down and the batter is ready to bat? He puts his hand down between his legs and wiggles his fingers which I first thought was to let the pitcher know that he "had to go". But he never does so it was probably just some more monkey business to fool the batter.

The next most fun to watch is the feller that is gettin' ready to bat when his turn comes. He stands out front where everybody can see him and gets a chance to show off. He always manages to turn around a couple of times to show the big number on his back and will pick up three or four bats, or slip a heavy iron ring around a bat to swing around to show what a he-man he is. So much for him.

Now let's take a look at the man all set to bat. He takes his good ol' time and comes a waltzin' up toward the plate like a prima donna gettin' ready to sing a song. First he adjusts his hat a few times, stoops over to tie a shoestring, or see if his battin' glove is on the right hand, lifts up a leg and hammers away on the heel, then feels to see if his shirt tail is tucked in. Then he will grab up a handful of dirt to rub on the bat handle and with extreme caution, approach the plate as if it were a loaded bear trap waitin' to grab him.

Finally after skuffin' in the dirt a few times he sticks out a dainty number fourteen size toe as close as he dares to the plate, hits the edge of the plate with his bat, flops himself around a few times, wriggles himself around quite a little, sticks his rump out as far as it will go, takes a quick peek up into the settin' seats to see if his gal is lookin', does his final machine gun style of spittin' as the umpire kneels. The tension is now terrific as we all hold our breath — but, nope, he ain't ready yet! For some unknown reason he lowers his bat, walks twenty feet away as the umpire comes to his feet and the audience lets out a near hurricane of pent-up air. However, before long he comes back and assumes his statue like stance. I already told you about him tryin' to hit the ball, didn't I?

Now, let's see what the pitcher does for excitement. Most of the pitchers are, or at least think they are "a breed apart" like Mister Lynch says about his big black longhorn bull who can trot down the golden isle of Tiffany's cut glass store without knockin' off a single priceless goblet, or even a demitasse. (I sure would like to be there with a hot-shot prod and watch the glass fly.) I think it is agreed that they do maintain that distinction, and very well too. A bulging jaw packed with Climax Cut-plug, maybe with a full set of shiny black whiskers as adornment, does indeed put them in the class "a breed apart". Ah, but a resemblance comes to mind. Is it to King Kong or perhaps to the famous "Wild Man of Borneo"? And at the moment of windup his beady little eyes sparkle and shine like a weasel peekin' in a hen house door and sap the nerves of the batter.

As he winds up for the kill, further distraction appears in the form of a well groomed, though slightly muscle bound leg gracefully extended and swept in an arc pointing at the twitching fingers between the legs of the catcher. The outcome of these distracting movements usually throws the pitcher off balance so that even the catcher is in doubt as to the final direction of the elusive little ball.

Then, of course, all managers use the time-honored black magic of switching the pitchers around. First a feller that throws the ball with his right hand, then one who throws with his left. This is to get the batter all mixed up so that he doesn't know where to stand, which hand to do the battin' with, and which side he is least likely to get hit. And none of those fellers now days can even throw a straight ball. Why the ball goes jumpin' around like crazy and the poor batter has got to guess where it will be when he takes a swipe at it. Most generally he hits nothin' but air, but he is always hopeful that he might accidently hit the ball sometime.

I've often wondered why so many roly-poly fellers are ball players. Why not more skinny fellers that can really run? Maybe you can remember quite a few years back, a feller by the name of

Mister Ruth? When he got kind of old, he got so fat he could scarcely break into a dog trot when he had to run. But Babe, everybody called him Babe, finally got the idea that all he had to do was knock the ball clear over the fence so he could take his good old time dog trottin' around the diamond.

Well I guess that's about enough talk on baseball, and I sure hope that from now on you will like to watch more baseball games since I have told you what to look for and laugh at the antics of the playin' fellers and don't lose any sleep over who beat who!

FOOTBALL

Now that we have had fun watchin' a baseball game, how about takin' a look at that other game called football? Maybe I can give you some of the fine points about that game, though I've never seen one except on TV. But as far as I can see I don't think it's near as good as baseball. In the first place they even play it in the middle of winter with a near foot of snow on the ground with the thermometer pushin' down around zero. I just can't see how anybody can be so foolish as to set on a board seat with sheepskin coats on, ear muffs, long johns likely, and of course mittens and overshoes and some folks even have a kerosene stove between their legs — just to watch a football game.

To start the doings going they have most anybody sing a song, if their singin' voice ain't froze up, while you stand there shiverin' with your hat off. Then about the time you get set, here comes what might look like a tribe of Indians on the war path. They mostly all got a round hard hat with bars across the front, maybe so they won't get their nose broke.

Folks always talk about a football eleven! Eleven my foot, if there ain't at least two or three hundred ready to play, I'll eat my shirt. And BIG? Why I never seen so many big fellers in my life. And if just being big ain't enough, they must stuff their shirts with pieces of orange crates or something, or else they are all as muscle lumpy as a jack mule. I'd even bet that some of them big bruisers are a full two axe handles across their shoulders and weigh close to a quarter of a ton. I expect they all drew numbers out of a hat to see who would wear a red shirt and the others wear some other color so they wouldn't be so apt to kill one another. I near forgot to mention that there is a fair sprinklin' of oddball fellers, not quite as big, and they all wear a striped coat clear down below their waist. I don't rightly know who they are, but anyway about all they do is toot on whistles and wave their arms and get in everybody's way. If I were the boss, I'd make them go and sit on the settin' seats with the other folks.

So now they are ready to play, or maybe I should say ready to fight. As soon as one of the oddballs toots on his whistle, each side gets into a tight little circle with their heads bent in like they were lookin' for something, or more than likely, sayin' their prayers which ain't such a bad idea. Now they all line up about four deep with the red shirts on one side and the blue shirts on the other side. But this time they mostly all get down on their knees, and if they don't pray again they are making a sad mistake 'cause it can be their very last chance before cashin' in their chips. Somebody blows on his whistle and you won't believe what I am going to tell you.

The whole bunch of them probably over a hundred includin' a few striped fellers, start runnin' every which way a slammin' and a bangin' into each other like they hated his guts. Why they slug, kick and scratch and jump on anybody with a different colored shirt on. But what gets me is that if a red shirt slugs a blue shirt, why the blue shirt ain't got guts enough to slug him back. Instead he just picks himself up an' goes bargin' and lookin' for somebody that's still on his feet!

You think that's bad? Just hang onto your seats, as so far they have just been warmin' up for the real battle. Now in the first place when the fight started, a feller about in the middle of the four lines has a football to hold. His idea being that he wants to get rid of it like it was a red hot poker. So he shoves it into the hands of some sucker who don't know what he's in for. Then the sucker looks for a hole to dash through and if he can't make it, he throws the ball as far as he can hoping somebody might catch it.

Now comes the sad part. If he ain't got time to throw the ball, then the poor fool is stuck with it and his only chance to see the next sunrise is to takeoff like a streak of lightin' for the far end of the corral. But as soon as he starts it looks like a herd of ruttin' buffalo ridin' his tail. The poor feller knows that should they catch him he will probably die a horrible death or at least will have to spend the rest of his life settin' on a street corner with a handful of pencils and a tin cup — and a little monkey if he can afford one.

But let's get to the worst and say that he gets caught. He has just about enough time to cast his eyes upwards when he is smashed down with from ten to fifteen or more bloodthirsty catamounts tryin' to get a strangle holt on him. Even after the poor feller has maybe cashed in his chips, they keep piling up on him. Why even the fellers that want in on the kill come bargin' in on a high lope and dive head first into the pile, or maybe jump clear over the pile to show what a good jumper he is.

Well soon as a striped coat man gets there he blows his whistle and they start diggin' in the pile to see if by chance there are any live remains. Of course if a feller is real lucky he just might escape with a leg or two broke. Now I hate to say it but it was the darn fool's fault cause he knew very well that if he took the ball he'd have no more chance than a short tailed bull in fly time.

Now let's say that with a lot of luck he did make it across the line at the back of the corral fence. Then it's a horse of a different color. He throws the ball on the ground as hard as he can, waves his arms, yells to high Heaven and no doubt thinks of all the nice offers he will get from pretty girls to come up for an early morning cup of tea.

Well! I hate to say it, but what with me bein' a perfectly honest and upright feller, I will have to admit that as long as quite a few folks go to such games they must be sort of interesting at that. So don't let me tell you how to have your fun.

Ballerina Bull

Awhile back me and my wife Eileen were takin' on a feed at the Cow Palace in Amado, Arizona where about forty or fifty years ago was a rodeo grounds at a now non-existent town by the name of Kinsley.

A big enlarged picture was hanging on the wall of the Cow Palace and it caught my eye as being the best bull ridin' picture I've ever seen. By nosin' around I found that the feller on the left in the picture is an old time rancher and still lives a hundred yards or so up the hill back of the Cow Palace.

The man on the hoss is Jim Mercer and he said that I could use it in my book. It's hard to believe that a near-ton-size animal could stand on one bent-over hoof and the end of his nose. (Thanks Jim and Eloise for lettin' me use the picture.)

"Ballerina Bull" — Cowboy on left is Jim Mercer.

The Grizzly and the Moose

Montana is, of course, widely known throughout the United States as being big game hunters paradise. Now me, well knowing of this reputation, and me being one of them fellers as don't pay too much attention to signs and rumors, took a chance on a big game hunt after the elusive mountain goat. Knowingly encroaching upon prime grizzly grounds might be described as having a dire, if not momentous, and fateful potential.

Well, there I was, fully at peace with the world and the beautiful panorama spread out before me as I blissfully threaded my way through the tangled lodgepole with an ever watchful eye scanning every suspicious object which could well be an ever equally watchful grizzly intent in the protection of her latest family members.

It almost seemed at that moment that my daydream had come true. Coming out of the tangled woods from a direction which placed me directly between mamma grizzly and her latest offspring came mamma herself. Red of eye and with a horrible roar of range, she hurled herself out of her hiding place and headed directly to the spot which, unfortunately for me, was the same spot on which I was standing.

It being out of season for grizzly bears, I couldn't use my gun. The grizzly, with only a half dozen more jumps to reach me, gave me but two options. I could either run or climb the tree under whose protective limbs I stood in mortal fear. Now what with me not having even a week to decide, and with another tree being at some distance away, I elected to leap three feet into the air and with one hand grasp a heaven sent limb.

As I tried to pull myself up out of reach, mamma Grizzly had now arrived and had other thoughts worthy of consideration. Without the necessity of stretching, she reached a hairy paw armed with 6" claws. With malice aforethought she elected to try a belt hold. This she did and as her armed claw came down, so did my belt, pants, one sock and one tightly laced hunting boot.

Well, there I was, perched safely on the limb and there she was, content to sit with watchful eye boring into mine.

After eyeing each other until far into the night which, of course, made it near impossible to even see each other, we both realized that something had to be done. I wanted to get home and Mrs. Grizzly wanted to feed her offspring who were now yowling their little heads off wondering where Ma was with her ever present supply of life-giving, calorie laden, mammary gland liquid refreshment.

So, around about midnight, I started things rolling by falling asleep and falling out of the tree. Unfortunately the limb on which I sat perched was exactly above Mrs. Grizzly, and I landed exactly between her shoulder blades at about the exact spot where a saddle would have been placed had I decided on trying that type of conveyance.

Taking advantage of every opportunity to stay aboard, I stayed on by grabbing a couple handfuls of dark brown fur and kicked myself that I had failed to wear my spurs when I started my hunt. Perhaps I had better let you know something more about this critter that I had just unceremoniously, and against my best judgement, mounted. Mrs. Grizzly wasn't of the common breed of somewhat pygmy size bears that one might encounter on the Kodiak Peninsula in Alaska. No, this one was a breed apart dating back perhaps to the days when Paul Bunyan roamed the wilds of our continent. Standing about 12 feet at the withers, she would have no doubt tipped the scale, if not actually breaking it, at roughly three ton give or take a few ounces. It is easy to see that what with her ample proportions I had plenty of room to compose my carcass and give me some of the homelike conveniences I was used to.

Her dark brown, foot long hair, though slightly odorous, permitted me to snuggle down with complete coverage from the cooling nightfall hovering slightly above the zero mark. Of course, the surging blood being pumped through the bear's body might well be likened to a steam heated 5th Avenue town house. I, of course, did not know where we were headed but I estimated from the draft of the wind and the nearly audible rhythmical high speed pumping of her heart, led me to believe that we were perhaps hitting all of 80 or more miles per hour.

Well, here we go, where to I don't know. Fortunately I had my pocket compass with me and with it I knew we passed, or rather climbed over the Rocky Mountains, the Big Horn Mountains and numerous less imposing obstructions until I knew that we were then entering the confines of Yellowstone Park where I was on a near speaking acquaintance with most of the denizens of the Park be they human or otherwise.

By this time it began to dawn on me why my steed had headed for Yellowstone Park. It being that she had undoubtedly been raised within the Park and figured that help could only be had in her own stamping grounds where relatives would come to her rescue.

Well, of course, this had to be all right with me, though I started to wonder where my help, if any, was to come from. Well, Mrs. Grizzly, being somewhat familiar with the trails and the by ways within the Park headed for the Old Faithful Inn.

Arriving at the front door at exactly the right moment, when someone opened the door to come out, we went in. We not only caused the raising of eyebrows, we raised the short hairs on the necks of all present. The Inn's employees were evidently prepared for such eventualities and within seconds mounted an offensive barrage of lead all the way from .22 pip squeaks to magnum projectiles & lead slugs including #00 and #4 buckshot. They were, of course, all aimed at the posterior of me and my steed. It was the only parts showing, and we made the 9 flights of log stairways, 14 steps to the jump.

The din was terrific, what with the noise of the guns coupled with my Comanche style war cry, the bear's throaty though terrifying and death defying growling to say nothing of the crying, screeching and general uproar on the part of the tourists at large.

However, at about that time, me and mamma bear had explored all 8 stories including the open log stairways which her downward dash to earth was made in from 15 to 20 step easy jumps as we recklessly managed the stairway turns other than the ones we missed entirely, and to save time, made gigantic leaps from one floor to another. As I later recalled, we had reduced our altitude from the 8th floor to ground level in exactly 4 and 1/2 jumps. The half jump was attained as the result of mamma bear having landed in a spread eagle belly flop which all but left her hopelessly prostrate and prayerfully on my part, out of the running.

Oh, no such luck! With broken staircase rails and steps raining down upon us and with the now popping and exploding guns each hopefully seeking a vital target, mamma bear gracefully cleared the huge vista window, which had been the pride and joy of the old hotel for many years. The window had been brought to the area on mule back to replace oiled paper panes, aptly named because it was for a fact painful to see through them.

Well, sir, we both came out of the fracas with only a few holes in our posterities (that means the back end). The bullets had practically given Ma Grizzly a haircut and there was mostly enough loose hair laying around that I could a' built me a first class nest. But me, I stood up about the time that the Mrs. jumped through the window. Just then is about the time when 4 shotguns went off at the same time and my posterity was really peppered!

I could feel most anywhere on my back and feel a #2 buckshot with sometimes a #4 which is twice as big. Fact is, had you stood back and taken a broadside, 'er I mean a back end view, you would probably have said I looked like a colander like Ma used to have. I don't expect you ain't never seen one of them colander things. They are about as big around as a soup kettle only it rounded on the bottom with 3 short legs to keep it from tipping over in case you wanted to set it down quick-like as when it got overly hot on you, or something.

Ma sure got took once when she was lookin' through the 1902 Sears Roebuck catalog. Well, sir, Mr. Roebuck put on a big sale one time. We heard one time that Mr. Sears didn't want to have a sale like that, but Mr. Roebuck won the flip and the 1902 catalog come out like Mr. Roebuck wanted.

Now you won't believe me if I tell you, but I am going to tell you anyway that right at this minute up home in Montana, where I got a house to live in, I have got one of them catalogs from 1902.

Toward the back end of the catalog they first had about 2 pages with different colored leaves so you could easy find them and on the first 2 pages they had all kinds of things and all priced at 2 cents each, then the next 2 pages were 3 cents each, and on up the line until you got to 8 cents each. Well, anyway, Ma could have bought one of them colander things on the 4 cent page, and she did. From the very beginning when we first got it brand new, it was plumb full of little holes about as big as a 14 or 15 gauge nail. We had a box of 8 and 10 penny nails, but the holes were a mite larger so they probably were made with a 14 or 15 gauge nail had there been any nails like that gauge.

What made Ma so mad was that the catalog page had set across the top "Cookin' Utensils — 4 Cents Each". Well, when Ma found she couldn't cook anything in a kettle that was full of holes she sent it back and told them about it and wanted them to either solder up the holes or send her money back. They said she could keep the colander. So that made it a very good deal and Ma was tickled pink to know that she got the colander for nothing.

But Ma was quite a genie, meaning that she was pretty ingenious. She found out that the kettle was good for something after all. She could put most anything in the colander and then take a wooden potato masher she always kept in a drawer and if she smashed hell out of whatever was in the colander, you would be surprised at what would come out of the holes.

But that ain't what I was going to tell you about. I really wanted to tell you that as long as Ma's colander had a lot of holes in it anyway, why Twitt and me used to use it for a target. Twitt would throw it up in the air and I would bang away at it with Pa's old double-barreled 10 gauge hammer gun which throwed seven #000 buckshot so hard we could knock a skunk or even a badger off his pins up to 10 rods or maybe more than that away.

Let's see now, I was going to tell you something but I forget now what it was, so let's get back to me and Mrs. Grizzly. Then we took off heading north which was about the same trail we used coming down a little earlier. Besides that I was getting awfully hungry and sure hoped we could get home pretty quick. I believe I did tell you that the Mrs. Bear I was ridin' on was 20 feet high, wasn't it? Well, anyway, that's close enough, but the reason I was glad she was that big was because about then we heard the gosh awfullest racket a'comin through the woods to the left.

Why it sounded like 3 or 4 freight trains all coupled together and we could see the trees crashing down and sticks a'flyin in the air and both me and Mrs. Grizzly near fainted from being scared.

Now if you will remember I told you before that a grizzly bear can't climb a tree. Well that might be all right in a book, but this grizzly I was ridin' on couldn't even read so she didn't pay any attention to what she could or couldn't do. Well, sir, she was so scared that quick as a flash she picked out one of the biggest trees there was and whether she could climb or not, up we went in 15 or 20 foot jumps until we finally ran out of trunk at 184 feet I think it was.

Then the sad part came. Mrs. Grizzly had never been that high up before and she got nervous and started shaking something terrible. It sure did rattle my teeth and darn if it didn't shake me off her back and down I went ass-over-teakettle. But as luck would have it, exactly at the right second, and just as the big critter went under the tree, I landed smack dab right between what I first thought was a couple of tree trunks sticking butt to butt, out sideways. Soon as I landed though, I could see they wasn't tree trunks but the biggest antlers I ever seen or rode on. I peeked over

the edge and guessed I must have been all of 30 or 40 feet in the air. Well, sir, there I was, worse off than on the bear, I figured. Besides that we were not even in high country, and a peek at my pocket gauge showed it to be 74 degrees below zero and dropping.

But you know that old moose feller was traveling so fast that the tree tops and branches he was knocking off was piled up around his antlers and I was able to pick up enough logs to build me a pretty fair size log shack with enough leaves and such to chink it near air tight. Better than that even, that old moose was travelin' so fast that he was kickin' up about everything including rocks and mud so's I was actually able to build up a not very good fireplace. With the 4 matches I found in the corner of one of my pockets I was even able to get me a fire started. Well, you can plain see that I was now about as well off as most folks and my only worry was how to get home.

I near forgot to mention that when Mrs. Grizzly and I jumped through the window back at the Old Faithful Inn a small 3" piece of the window got caught in my coat pocket. I fixed this up in the wall like a little window so's I could peek out and see where we was goin'.

Don't you suppose that about 2:30 in the afternoon after leaving Old Faithful the week before, darned if I didn't see Roaring Lion Box Canyon. About half way up the canyon was where my wife and 3 little kid fellers lived. Quick as a flash I knew I had to figure how to get my moose to stop and then it dawned on me. If I could steer him up the box canyon far enough to where the canyon got narrower, why sooner or later his horns would hit on either side and stop him cold. So I picked up a saplin' about 10 feet long and swiped him across the jaw and got him steered up the canyon. Well, sir, when we got fairly close to our log shack I stepped outside of my little shack on the moose and whistled my danger signal to my wife which meant to her — danger, get your gun. I could see her high-tail it for her trusty rifle and as we went astraddle of our house she ups and empties her gun straight up into Mr. Moose's heart spot. Mom musta' hit him smack dab in the heart 'cause after about another 100 rods or so the tip ends of the moose's antlers started a' scrapin' on the sides of the canyon and he finally keeled over — hanging part way up 'cause his antlers held him up. You have probably already figured that all I had to do was crawl out on the moose's antlers and step off onto the mountain side and get home in time for supper.

I am not even going to take the time to tell you how we went about it to make use of an old gold mine shaft which goes into the side of the mountain so far it's hard froze all of the time. All we had to do was quarter up the moose and within 30 days with 162 of our neighbors helpin', we packed the mine cave near full with moose meat. We have scarce made a dent in that meat even though it has now been, let's see, from 1921 to now . . . would be an even 61 years or so, I believe.

Just one more surprise and I will button up this true story. I didn't know it then, but when I fell out of the tree onto the horns of the moose, why Mrs. Grizzly musta' fell out too and she was ridin' on the back end of the moose which is why we didn't see each other until when I got home.

Don't you suppose that a couple of days later here comes Mrs. Grizzly and her two little cub fellers trailing along behind her. It seems that I must have lost my white handkerchief somewhere along the line and Mrs. Grizzly found it. When she and her two little cub fellers came to our door, why she had this white handkerchief in her mouth as a signal of peace and I was so overcome with joy and love that we not only had her and the 2 little cub fellers stay for supper, we extended them our heartfelt thanks and perpetual permission to help themselves to our moose cache in the mountain. In fact, she is known far and wide as the "keeper of the moose". Now as I said at the very beginning — I was going to tell you a true story and I am so glad to have actually done so, or at least tried to.

Anytime you wish, you can talk to the Montana Power Company and they will tell you that from then on, they ran their power lines through these wide paths through the woods that the moose's antlers had cleared for them. Nearly wherever you go in the Western States you will see those paths with the power wires going through them. Whether from Butte to Helena, Billings to Roundup, Hamilton to Miles City, when you see those paths you will surely remember when Frosty took his ride back in 1921. This ride pales Paul Revere's ride into insignificance.

So long and I hope you enjoyed this true story, I mean . . . tale.

A Hunting Story

I remember one time me and another feller was coming home from hunting antelope down around Baker and on our way home we stopped in a little town for a cup of java. A lot of fellers were settin' around on stools drinkin' coffee and all had red hats on. We pricked up our ears when we found it was open season on deer, so we asked a gent should he know where we might pick up a buck or so.

He told us to go up the trail three or four miles, turn left another couple of miles and should we hunt out a couple of draws, why we might flush us a buck or two. Well, sir, we no mor'n got up towards the foot of a draw when old eagle-eye Norm says "whoa up" an' points to a clump of brush about 200 yards up the draw.

"Frosty" he says, "I think I seen something move in the left hand side of that brush." By that time I was squintin' through my 8 power Carl Zeiss binoculars — serial number 1734090 — an' whispers to Norm; "two of 'em!" "The hell," he says as we ease ourselves out the car doors an' squat down lookin' like "Billy can and Billy can't," little statues us kids used to have showing kids settin' on pots. I could see two big racks peekin' out of the brush near level with each other.

"I'll take the top one," I whispers, knowing that I had only about 3 or 4 inches of meat to aim at over the neck of the bottom one. I might say here and now that what's-his-name and me ain't fellers as would shoot fish in a barrel, but thinkin' it over for a small second or less, we were careful like easing a cartridge in an' drawin' us a part lung-full of air and lettin' out a small half of it or less expectin' them to evaporate into thin air with any more diddlin' and daddlin' around by we two.

Careful-like, we draws down on them. Norm with his old 06 and me with a brand spankin' new Winchester from which when I first got it I sawed off about 4 inches from the barrel, front end of course. (Reason bein' I ain't pretty tall and with a 24 inch barrel it sort of drags in the dirt.) What with a 2 x 7 Redfield scope perched on top, I'm not even going to try tellin' what I could do with it. But toss a small tin can in the air and I wouldn't even shoot lessen' there was an "i" I could dot.

Then BANG, BANG with a couple of echoes verberatin' and reverberatin' up and down the draw like they never would stop. An' we, as nervous as our hired-girl when she got part of her anatomy caught in the wringer, jumped to our feet as a passel of dogs up the side of the hill to our right took up their favorite brand of greetin'. At the same time old eagle-eye Norm spots a small house in the edge of the woods and yells, "Frosty, there's a house up there so let's get to hell out of here!"

We wasn't about to leave without our bucks so we jumps in the jeep an' pours ourselves up the little rise an' again we near fainted when a 5 or 6 strand bobwire fence jumped up before our eyes with the two bucks about fifty feet inside of the fence. We could easy see that all wires, high and low, were stretched "tighter than a little bull's butt in flytime." Only a gopher or an eagle could get through that fence.

We could see a few horns stickin' up out of the weeds and what's-his-name figured maybe we could lasso a horn or two. We tied two 30 foot hemp ropes together and took about a half a dozen tries each but all we could come up with was a few weeds.

"How in hell are we goin' to get them," Norm yells. "Get in," I tells him and we skidded the jeep up alongside of the fence. "Get on top an' jump over," I tells him. He makes it in one jump an' ties one end of the rope around both sets of horns while I anchor the other end to the jeep. "Let 'er rip," he says as I pull back on the four-wheel lever and the dust flies as I take off.

The dogs were getting into better voice right along. Norm was runnin' right behind the caravan when of a sudden five or maybe eight horn tips caught on the bottom wire and held fast. Norm managed to tuck the horns under the wire and we were ready to go again. It then dawned on me that poor old Norm would still be inside the fence.

The Devil and me near decided to let what's-his-name take his own chances but my heart went out to his family of a fine wife, two sons and a right purty 16-year-old daughter. Me bein' quick-witted (spent three years in college learnin' to be a half-wit) I said, "Norm, I'll pull the deer through till only their back legs show; then you lay flat on yore belly or yore back if you want, an' freeze onto a leg or two an' I'll pull yuh under the fence. It might be high enough if yuh let out yore wind.

He froze onto a back laig and I tromped on the pedal and a well-worn clutch jumped me about four feet as I heard what's-his-name let out a yelp. I thought maybe I had disemboweled poor old Norm. But he was a tough old rooster and about all the damage I could see was his big belt buckle had caught on the wire and had scraped his pants clear down over his boot tops. There was a fair amount of blood on his belly an' I was scared that I might a' pulled his belly button out or something.

Then to top it all off we hears a man yelling and dogs raisin' hell as man and beasts came roarin' out of the woods. Me and what's-his-name quick-like gathered up our belongings and with the horns a-gougin' in the dirt we "took off like a cut cat" down the road and around a bend figurin' we had time to at least gut the bucks afore he could catch up with us — or get hisself a horse.

Some folks think that a cowboy's life was *romantic!*

Lone Cowboy

Forty miles from town — twenty miles to the home ranch — a 10 x 10 ft. log, sod or dugout line shack — firewood out back — spring fed creek close by — string of broncs — a few hundred cows to nurse — grub enough to last a month — a 30-30 and a 45 (cartridges for both) — and all for thirty and found.

For entertainment the cowboy has some of nature's hardest and meanest punches - sudden storms such as wind, snow, hail, lightening, heat, freezing weather, drought, prairie fires, bog holes, badger and prairie dog holes, as well as his own possible ailments such as colds, toothaches, bellyaches, this and that as well as LONELINESS.

His job is COW, from top to bottom, up and down, sidewise, slantwise, crosswise, front and back. A mail order catalog is his means of keepin' up on pretty gals. Yup, I think he is "a breed apart".

Cowboy Laundry

On a typical homestead, as a rule, a cowboy had only one shirt. It was the custom to pick a nice spring day and rinse clothes in a nearby creek. During winter months socks were worn near night and day, so required little or no attention. A red bandana was worn around the neck. The normal use of it as a handkerchief was more appropriately and sanitarily taken care of with a right and left hand blast followed by a coat sleeve swipe from cuff to elbow.

Undershirt and drawers were likewise worn steadily from the first snowfall to far into the summer. It is interesting to note that during a normal summer's use, a pair of Levis would become so saturated with sweat and grease that when removed at night, could be stood up rather than lay in a heap.

During winters with shack temperature usually below freezing it was near impossible to don one's Levis until they had thawed out. But usually with Levis parked standing, it was only a matter of stepping into them. A good reason why a cowboy was always looking for a wife.

A Cowboy's Christmas Prayer

(by S. Omar Barker)

I ain't much good at prayin'
    and You may not know me, Lord -
I ain't much seen in churches
    where they preach Thy Holy Word,
But You may have observed me
    out here on the lonely plains,
A-lookin' after cattle,
    feelin' thankful when it rains.

Admirin' Thy great handiwork,
    the miracle of grass,
Aware of Thy kind spirit
    in the way it comes to pass
That hired men on horseback
    and the livestock that we tend
Can look up at the stars at night
    and know we've got a Friend.

So here's ol' Christmas comin' on,
    remindin' us again
Of Him whose coming brought good will
    into the hearts of men.
A cowboy ain't no preacher, Lord,
    but if You'll hear my prayer,
I'll ask as good as we have got
    for all men everywhere.

Don't let no hearts be bitter, Lord,
    don't let no child be cold.

Make easy beds for them that's sick
    and them that's weak and old.
Let kindness bless the trail we ride
    no matter what we're after
And sorter keep us on Your side,
    in tears as well as laughter.

I've seen old cows a-starvin',
    and it ain't no happy sight;
Please don't leave no one hungry, Lord,
    on Thy good Christmas night -
No man, no child, no woman,
    and no critter on four feet -
I'll aim to do my best
    to help You find 'em chuck to eat.

I'm just a sinful cowpoke, Lord -
    ain't got no business prayin' -
But still I hope You'll ketch
    a word or two of what I'm sayin':
We speak of Merry Christmas, Lord -
    I reckon You'll agree
There ain't no Merry Christmas
    for nobody that ain't free.

So one thing more I'll ask You, Lord:
    just help us what You can
To save some seeds of freedom
    for the future sons of man.

Friend

(Author unknown)

I'd like to be the sort of friend
    that you have been to me
I'd like to be the help that you've
    been always glad to be.

I'd like to mean as much to you
    each minute of the day
As you have meant old friend of mine
    to me along the way.

I'm wishing at this Christmas time
    that I could but repay
A portion of the gladness
    that you've strewn along my way.

And could I have one wish this year
    this only would it be,
I'd like to be the sort of friend
    that you have been to me.

Who Will Take Grandma?

(Author unknown)

Who will take Grandma? Who will it be?
    All of us want her, I'm sure you'll agree.
Let's call a meeting, let's gather the clan,
    Let's get it settled . . . as soon as we can.

In such a large family there's certainly one
    Willing to give her a place in the sun.
Strange how we thought she'd never wear out
    But you see how she walks . . arthritis, no doubt.

Her eye sight is fading, her memory is dim
    She's apt to insist on the silliest whim.
When persons get older they become such a care
    She must have a home . . the question is where!

Remember the days when she used to be spry . .
    Baked her own cookies and made her own pies,
Helped us with our lessons and mended our seams,
    Kissed away troubles and mended our dreams.

Wonderful Grandma, we all love her so,
    Isn't it dreadful she has no place to go!
One little corner is all she would need,
    A shoulder to cry on, her Bible to read.

A chair by the window, the sun shining through
    Some pretty spring flowers, still covered with dew.
Who'll warm her with love so she won't mind the cold?
    Who will take Grandma now that she's so old?

What! Nobody wants her? . . Oh yes, there is one
    Willing to give her a place in the sun
Where she won't have a worry, or wonder, or doubt
    And she won't have a problem to bother about.

Pretty soon now, God will give her a bed
    But who will dry our tears when Grandma is dead?

The Shooting of Dan McGrew

(by Robert Service)

A bunch of the boys were whooping it up
    in the Malamute saloon;
The kid that handles the music box
    was hitting a rag-time tune;
Back of the bar, in a solo game,
    sat Dangerous Dan McGrew,
And watching his luck was his light-o'-love,
    the lady that's known as Lou.
When out of the night, which was fifty below,
    and into the din and glare,
There stumbled a miner fresh from the creeks,
    dog-dirty, and loaded for bear.
He looked like a man with a foot in the grave
    and scarcely the strength of a louse,
Yet he tilted a poke of dust on the bar,
    and he called for drinks for the house.
There was none could place the stranger's face,
    though we searched ourselves for a clue;
But we drank to his health and the last to drink
    was Dangerous Dan McGrew.
There's men that somehow just grip your eyes,
    and hold them hard like a spell;
And such was he and he looked to me like a
    man who had lived in hell;
With a face most hair, and the dreary stare
    of a dog whose day is done,
As he watered the green stuff in his glass,
    and the drops fell one by one.
Then I got to figgering who he was,
    and wondering what he'd do,
And I turned my head - and there watching him
    was the lady that's known as Lou.
His eyes went rubbering round the room,

and he seemed in a kind of daze,
'Til at last that old piano fell in the way
of his wandering gaze.
The rag-time kid was having a drink;
there was no one else on the stool,
So the stranger stumbles across the room,
and flops down there like a fool.
In a buckskin shirt that was glazed with dirt
he sat, and I saw him sway;
Then he clutched the keys with his talon hands -
my God! but that man could play.

Were you ever out in the Great Alone,
when the moon was awful clear,
And the icy mountains hemmed you in
with a silence you most could hear;
With only the howl of a timber wolf,
and you camped there in the cold,
A half-dead thing in a stark, dead world,
clean mad for the muck called gold;
While high overhead, green, yellow and red,
the North Lights swept in bars
Then you've a hunch what the music meant . . .
hunger and night and the stars.

And hunger not of the belly kind
that's banished with bacon and beans,
But the gnawing hunger of lonely men
for a home and all that it means;
For a fireside far from the cares that are
four walls and a roof above;
But oh! so cramfull of cozy joy
and crowned with a woman's love -
A woman dearer than all the world,
and true as Heaven is true -
(God! how ghastly she looks through her rouge, -
the lady that's known as Lou.)
Then on a sudden the music changed,
so soft that you scarce could hear;
But you felt that your life had been looted clean
of all that it once held dear;

That someone had stolen the woman you loved,
    that her love was a devil's lie;
That your guts were gone, and the best for you
    was to crawl away and die.
'Twas the crowning cry of a heart's despair,
    and it thrilled you through and through -
"I guess I'll make it a spread misere",
    said Dangerous Dan McGrew.

The music almost died away . .
    then it burst like a pent-up flood;
And it seemed to say, "Repay, repay,"
    and my eyes were blind with blood.
The thought came back of an ancient wrong,
    and it stung like a frozen lash,
And the lust awoke to kill, to kill . . .
    then the music stopped with a crash,
And the stranger turned, and his eyes they burned
    in a most peculiar way;
In a buckskin shirt that was glazed with dirt
    he sat, and I saw him sway;
Then his lips went in a kind of grin,
    and he spoke, and his voice was calm,
And "Boys," says he, "you don't know me,
    and none of you care a damn;
But I want to state, and my words are straight,
    and I'll bet my poke they're true,
That one of you is a hound of hell . . .
    and that one is Dan McGrew."

Then I ducked my head, and the lights went out,
    and two guns blazed in the dark,
And a woman screamed, and the lights went up,
    and two men lay stiff and stark.
Pitched on his head, and pumped full of lead,
    was Dangerous Dan McGrew,
While the man from the creeks lay clutched to
    the breast of the lady that's known as Lou.

These are the simple facts of the case,
    and I guess I ought to know.

They say that the stranger was crazed with "hootch,"
  and I'm not denying it's so.
I'm not so wise as the lawyer guys,
  but strictly between us two -
The woman that kissed him and - pinched his poke -
  was the lady that's known as Lou.

Courtesy of DODD MEAD & COMPANY, New York

The Cremation of Sam McGee

(by Robert Service)

There are strange things done in the midnight sun
  by the men who moil for gold;
The Arctic trails have their secret tales
  that would make your blood run cold;
The Northern Lights have seen queer sights,
  but the queerest they ever did see
Was that night on the marge of Lake Lebarge
  I cremated Sam McGee.

Now Sam McGee was from Tennessee,
  where the cotton blooms and blows.
Why he left his home in the South to roam
  'round the Pole, God only knows.
He was always cold, but the land of gold
  seemed to hold him like a spell;
Though he'd often say in his homely way
  that "he'd sooner live in Hell".

On a Christmas Day we were mushing our way
  over the Dawson Trail.
Talk of your cold! Through the parka's fold
  it stabbed like a driven nail.
If our eyes we'd close, then the lashes froze
  'til sometimes we couldn't see;
It wasn't much fun, but the only one
  to whimper was Sam McGee.

And that very night, as we lay packed tight

in our robes beneath the snow,
And the dogs were fed, and the stars o'er head
    were dancing heel and toe,
He turned to me, and "Cap", says he,
    "I'll cash in this trip, I guess;
And if I do, I'm asking that you
    won't refuse my last request."
Well, he seemed so low that I couldn't say no;
    then he says with a sort of moan
"It's the cursed cold, and it's got right hold
    'til I'm chilled clean through to the bone.
Yet, 'taint being dead - - - it's my awful dread
    of the icy grave that pains;
So I want you to swear that foul or fair
    you'll cremate my last remains."

A pal's last need is a thing to heed
    so I swore I would not fail;
And we started on at the streak of dawn
    but God! he looked ghastly pale.
He crouched on the sleigh, and he raved all day
    of his home in Tennessee;
And before nightfall, a corpse was all
    that was left of Sam McGee.

There wasn't a breath in that land of death,
    and I hurried, horror-driven,
With a corpse half hid, that I couldn't get rid,
    because of a promise given;
It was lashed to the sleigh, and it seemed to say:
    "You may tax your brawn and brains,
But you promised true, and it's up to you
    to cremate those last remains."

Now a promise made is a debt unpaid,
    and the trail has its own stern code.
In the days to come, though my lips were dumb,
    In my heart, how I cursed that load.
In the long, long night, by the lone fire light,
    While the huskies, round in a ring,
Howled out their woes to the homeless snows -
    O God! how I loathed the thing.

And every day that quiet clay
    seemed to heavy and heavier grow;
And on I went, though the dogs were spent,
    and the grub was getting low;
The trail was bad, and I felt half mad,
    but I swore I would not give in;
And I'd often sing to the hateful thing,
    and it hearkened with a grin.

'Til I came to the marge of Lake Lebarge,
    and a derelict there lay;
It was jammed in the ice, but I saw in a trice,
    it was called the "Alice May".
And I looked at it, and I thought a bit,
    and I looked at my frozen chum;
Then "Here," said I, with a sudden cry,
    "is my cre-ma-tor-eum".

Some planks I tore from the cabin floor,
    and I lit the boiler fire;
Some coal I found that was lying around,
    and I heaped the fuel higher;
The flames just soared, and the furnace roared -
    such a blaze you seldom see;
And I burrowed a hole in the glowing coal,
    and I stuffed in Sam McGee.

Then I made a hike, for I didn't like
    to hear him sizzle so;
And the Heavens scowled, and the huskies howled,
    and the wind began to blow.
It was icy cold, but the hot sweat rolled
    down my cheeks, and I don't know why;
And the greasy smoke in an inky cloak
    went streaking down the sky.

I do not know how long in the snow
    I wrestled with grisly fear;
But the stars came out and they danced about
    ere again I ventured near;
I was sick with dread, but I bravely said:

"I'll just take a peep inside,
I guess he's cooked, and it's time I looked" . . .
    then the door I opened wide.
And there sat Sam, looking cool and calm,
    in the heart of the furnace roar;
And he wore a smile you could see a mile,
    and he said: "Please close that door.
It's fine in here, but I greatly fear
    you'll let in the cold and storm - - -
Since ah' left Plumtree, down in Tennessee,
    it's the first time ah've been warm."
There are strange things done in the midnight sun
    by the men who moil for gold;
The Arctic trails have their secret tales
    that would make your blood run cold;
The Northern Lights have seen queer sights,
    but the queerest they ever did see,
Was that night on the marge of Lake Lebarge,
    I cremated Sam McGee.

Courtesy of DODD MEAD & COMPANY, New York

Frosty doing a little cogitatin'.

More Cowboy Sayin's

- He was lappin' up liquor like a fired cowhand.
- He serves a free snake with every drink.
- The biggest snake I ever saw without the aid of likker.
- He suffered from a disease called bottle fever.
- Thet likker done et its way plumb to my boot heels.
- It don't take backbone to belly up to a bar.
- A corkscrew never pulled a man out of a hole.
- Yuh might be the best bar-dog as ever waved a bar-rag, but I don't crave yuh a spittin' tobacco juice in the bottle to give it a good color.
- Mad 'nough to chomp a chunk out of a axe.
- As sullen as a sore headed dog.
- Cold as a banker's heart.
- She was as homeless as a poker-chip.
- A loose mare is always lookin' for a new pasture.
- Most men are like a bobwire fence — they all have their good points.
- "Oh, is that you, Maw?" said the little porcupine as he backed into a cactus.
- As thirsty as a mudhen on a tin roof.
- So blind he can't see through a bobwire fence.
- Had as much chance as a rabbit in a hound's mouth.
- Tight as a woodtick on a dog's tail.
- Tongue hangin' out a foot an' forty inches.
- When he bellered, "Scat!" they all hunted their holes.
- Mean 'nough to have a reserved seat in hell.
- Snorin' fit to shake the ticks out of his blankets.
- As nervous as a hen at a mass meetin' of coyotes.
- Scratchin' his feet like a centipede with the chilblains.
- Had a voice that would drive a wolf to suicide.
- Fogged it out of the country like a turpentined cat.
- He skeedaddled out of town on a quick-bought hoss.
- Every time he gets into trouble he tries to pull hisself out by gettin' down on his prayer-bones an' taffy'n the Lord up.
- As lean as a desert grasshopper.
- So quiet you could hear daylight coming.
- Silent as a tree full of owls.

Scott Nelson & Frosty

The art work in this book is in memory of my friend, Brendan J. Hopfauf.

Scott Nelson,

Illustrator

Scott the Illustrator

It may be a little unusual for the author of a book to write a story about his illustrator. Well, I am going to do this as I feel that I probably know him mostly as well as his Ma does. Yuh see, his folks and my folks used to own cattle ranches not too many miles apart startin' back around 1903 when we bought our Diamond N Ranch.

Of course, I am quite a bit older than Scott what with me bein' in the nineties and Scott just a young feller. We Potters no longer own the old Diamond N but Scott and his family still live on their same old spread. I scarce knew of Scott until a few years ago when he wrote me wanting to buy a copy of each of my books, ***Cowboy Slang*** and ***Whoa . . . Yuh Sonsabitches.***

From then on every time he wrote me a letter he would draw a picture on the letter or on the back of the envelope. From the very beginning his progress was so pronounced that I had to realize that here is another Charlie Russell in the making. Now Charlie didn't just paint a horse, Charlie near made that horse talk. Scott has that knack which he has learned through his own efforts. I say give this young feller enough rope and he probably won't hang himself, but it might get a lot of his pictures hanged!

Sometime back my wife, Eileen, and I visited Scott on their ranch which brought back visions of my old ranch days. Scott says he does most of his sketching and painting during the winter with the gauge hoverin' between 40 and 50 below. For the past few hunting seasons, time permitting, Scott has worked with big game hunting outfits in the Bob Marshall Wilderness Area in the northwest corner of Montana.

He says that the action he encountered in the wilds will be invaluable for his art. He came home with some bear and elk meat and the prime pelt from the bear. But he forgot to mention did he shoot the bear, or did he use his ten-inch toad sticker which he knows how to use when the chips are down.

So is it any wonder that I picked Scott to do my art work? Yup, I like that young feller first-class.

Frosty the Author

Edgar Reed Potter

Author Edgar (Frosty) Potter was born in Elma, Iowa on June 12, 1895. He was one of eight children in a family consisting of seven boys and one girl. His father, Henry W. Potter, came West with the Potter family from North Conway, New Hampshire in about 1865 and settled in Howard County, Iowa where he married Cora Louise Pooler.

In 1903 the Potters again moved westward, this time to North Dakota where Henry purchased range land. The Diamond N Ranch was located thirty miles south of Mandan and fifteen miles west of the Missouri River. On that sparse land they scratched out a living and endured the bitterly tough winters. Mandan was the closest place for food and supplies. Visitors were few. Indians from the nearby Sioux Indian Reservation freely roamed the countryside and on occasion would come to the house. A congenial relationship existed between all parties.

While living on the ranch, Frosty stepped on a pitchfork and drove the tine into an anklebone leaving him with blood poisoning and a permanently stiff ankle. In 1909 Frosty's father was killed in a railroad accident which occurred while taking his cattle to market in Chicago.

After that Cora was left to raise the children. She eventually sold the ranch, but remained in the area and later became postmistress in the small town of Breien just six miles south of the Diamond N. Grandma Cora's home in Breien was for many years the site of family gatherings, hunting trips, and vacations.

Frosty attended the Dakotah Business College in Fargo and then landed a job with the Northwestern Bell Telephone Co. He married Anne Myklebust and they settled down to raise their three boys. (Gordon, the oldest, was killed in North Africa during World War II.)

Frosty and Anne retired and moved to Hamilton, Montana. They spent their winters in Mesa, Arizona and were among the first of the modern-day "Snowbirds". They moved again to Fallbrook, California and then back to Hamilton where Anne died of cancer in 1977.

In 1983 Frosty married Eileen Wiles. They lived several years on Eileen's small "ranch" with a view of Mt. Lemmon in the Coronado National Forest near Tucson, Arizona.

Frosty and Eileen are now living in a retirement center in Tucson and enjoy visiting Eileen's family near Columbus, Ohio and Frosty's sons (Jack and his wife Mary Lou who live in Tucson and Tom and his wife Phyllis who live in California.) Frosty looks forward to June of 1995 when he will be 100 years old!

Eileen Potter

Also by "Frosty" Potter!

Cowboy Slang *will complete your education in cowboy lore! Don't be a tenderfoot - climb on and ride with "Frosty" and the REAL cowboys!*

COWBOY SLANG

Lingo of the American West captured in 2000 phrases and expressions—colorful, humorous, earthy, raunchy! Includes horse and cattle terms, barbwire names, cattle brands. Illustrated by Ron Scofield. Written by Edgar "Frosty" Potter.

5 1/2 x 8 1/2 — 128 Pages . . . $5.95

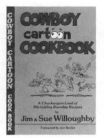

ORDER BLANK

GOLDEN WEST PUBLISHERS

☼ 4113 N. Longview Ave. • Phoenix, AZ 85014

602-265-4392 • **1-800-658-5830** • FAX 602-279-6901

Qty	Title	Price	Amount
	Arizona Adventure	6.95	
	Arizona Museums	9.95	
	Arizona Outdoor Guide	6.95	
	Best Barbecue Recipes	5.95	
	Cactus Country	6.95	
	Chili-Lovers Cook Book	5.95	
	Cowboy Cartoon Cookbook	5.95	
	Cowboy Country Cartoons	4.50	
	Cowboy Slang	5.95	
	Cowboys Talk Right Purty!	5.95	
	Ghost Towns in Arizona	6.95	
	Horse Trails in Arizona	9.95	
	In Old Arizona	6.95	
	Old West Adventures in Arizona	5.95	
	Quest for the Dutchman's Gold	6.95	
	Salsa Lovers Cook Book	5.95	
	Snakes and other Reptiles of the SW	9.95	
	Texas Cook Book	5.95	
	Tequila Cook Book	7.95	
	Wild West Characters	6.95	
Add $2.00 to total order for shipping & handling			$2.00

☐ My Check or Money Order Enclosed. . . . . $ _____

☐ MasterCard   ☐ VISA

Acct. No.   Exp. Date

Signature

Name   Telephone

Address

City/State/Zip   **Call for FREE catalog**

1/95   MasterCard and VISA Orders Accepted ($20 Minimum)

Talk Purty!

This order blank may be photo-copied.